Exclusive Distributors:
Music Sales Limited
8/9 Frith Street, London W1V 5TZ, England.
Music Sales Pty Limited
120 Rothschild Avenue, Rosebery, NSW 2018, Australia.

Book design by Michael Bell Design.
Music arranged and processed by Barnes Music Engraving.

This book © Copyright 1993 by Wise Publications
Order No. AM91219
ISBN 0-7119-3462-2

Music Sales' complete catalogue lists thousands of titles and is
free from your local music shop, or direct from Music Sales Limited.
Please send a cheque/postal order for £1.50 for postage to:
Music Sales Limited, Newmarket Road, Bury St. Edmunds, Suffolk IP33 3YB.

Your Guarantee of Quality:
As publishers, we strive to produce every book to the highest commercial standards.
The music has been freshly engraved and the book has been carefully designed to
minimise awkward page turns and to make playing from it a real pleasure.
Throughout, the printing and binding have been planned to ensure a sturdy,
attractive publication which should give years of enjoyment.

If your copy fails to meet our high standards, please inform us and
we will gladly replace it.

Unauthorised reproduction of any part of this publication by any means
including photocopying is an infringement of copyright.

Printed in the United Kingdom by
Caligraving Limited, Thetford, Norfolk.

Wise Publications
London / New York / Paris / Sydney / Copenhagen / Madrid

Playtime for Recorder
Traditional Folk Tunes

Blow The Man Down 8
Cherry Ripe 10
Danny Boy (Londonderry Air) 14
Drink To Me Only With Thine Eyes 16
Early One Morning 9
Greensleeves 18
Hearts Of Oak 20
Home Sweet Home 22
On Ilkley Moor Baht'at 24
Scarborough Fair 25
The Ash Grove 26
The Vicar Of Bray 28
There Is A Tavern In The Town 30

traditional folk tunes
Another fun-sized songbook for young recorder players

Recorder Care

Both wooden and plastic instruments need delicate, although different, care if they are to last, and remain in excellent playing condition.

Wooden Recorders

1. Play the instrument only at room temperature.
This can be achieved by holding the instrument under the armpit before playing.

2. After each playing session the recorder should be taken apart and dried with a swab.

3. Break in a new instrument gradually: twenty minutes at a time for the first two weeks, and thirty minutes for approximately the next two weeks.

4. Do not expose the recorder to extreme temperature changes.

5. Use cork grease for easier assembly of the instrument, and to avoid drying out the corks.

6. Oil the bore lightly approximately every six months.

Plastic Recorders

1. Play the instrument only at room temperature.
This can be achieved by holding the instrument under the armpit before playing.

2. After playing, dry the interior of the instrument with a swab.

3. Wipe the exterior with a lint-free cloth.

4. The recorder should be washed occasionally with a mild, gentle soap in warm water, rinsed, and dried.

The Recorder

The recorder is a vertical flute with a beak-shaped mouthpiece into which a block (fipple) is inserted to form a windway.

Recorder Range

Most recorders today are patterned after instruments of the Baroque period. They have a full chromatic range of two octaves and a minor third, and a strong reedy tone quality.

The descant recorder sounds one octave higher than notated, and its range is:

Descant

Basic Recorder Technique

1. Hold the recorder with the left hand on top and the right hand at the bottom.

2. Place the recorder between the lips and in front of the teeth.

3. Cover the thumb-hole with the left thumb at a 45° angle to the recorder. This step is extremely important, because an incorrect thumb position causes a poor hand position.

4. Keeping the thumb-hole covered, cover the first hole at the top with the first finger of the left hand. Recorder holes should be covered with the cushions (pads) of the fingers.

5. No finger pressure is necessary.

6. Rest the recorder on the right thumb, between the fourth and fifth holes.

7. Fingers which are not being used at this stage should remain slightly above but not touching the holes.

8. Bring the corners of the mouth gently and slightly forward.

9. Exhale gently into the recorder and think of making a silent "daah" sound.

10. Always play softly and tongue (silent "daah") gently.

11. The lips and fingers should be relaxed at all times.

12. Tongue every note. Do not slur from note to note.

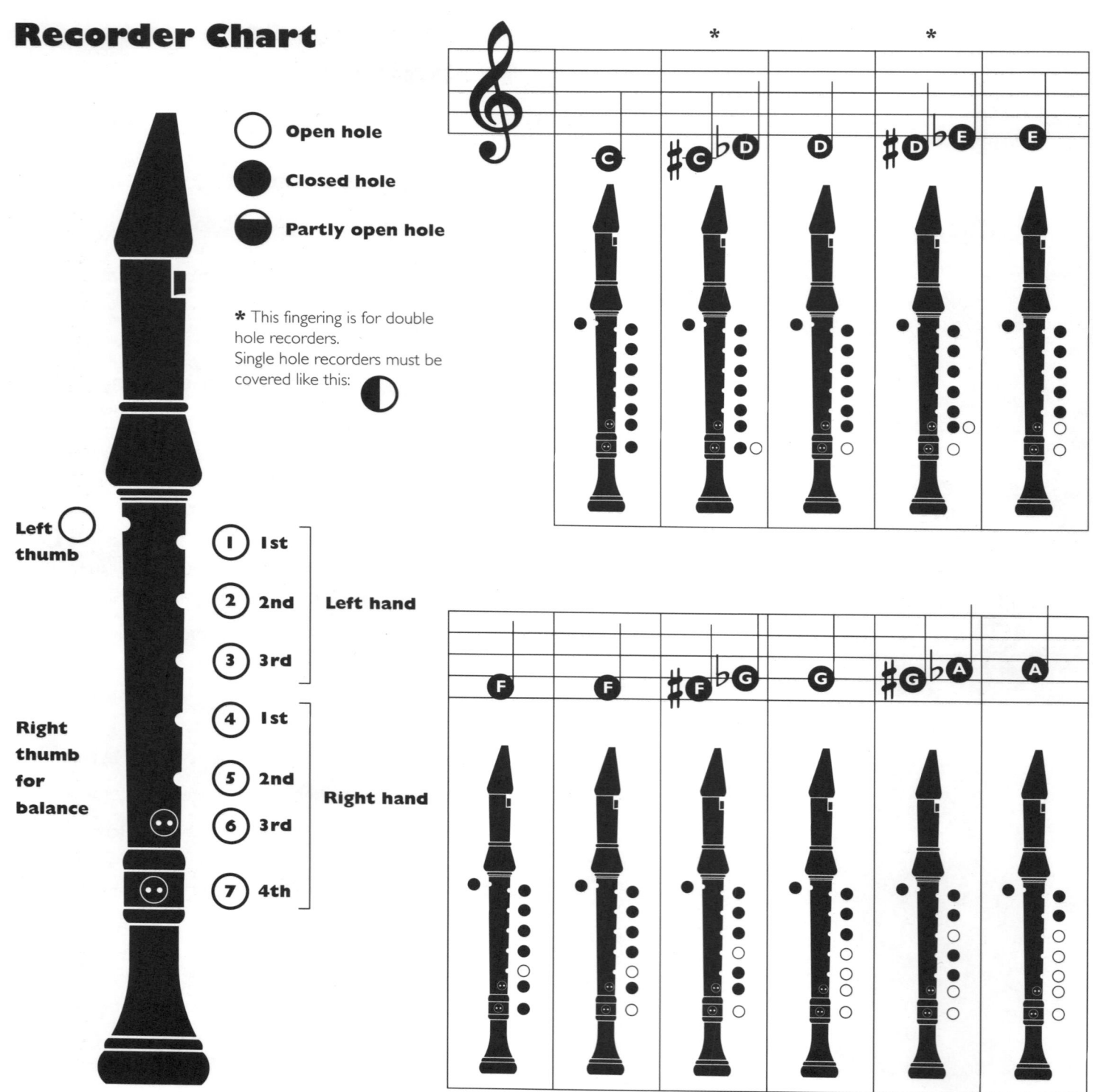

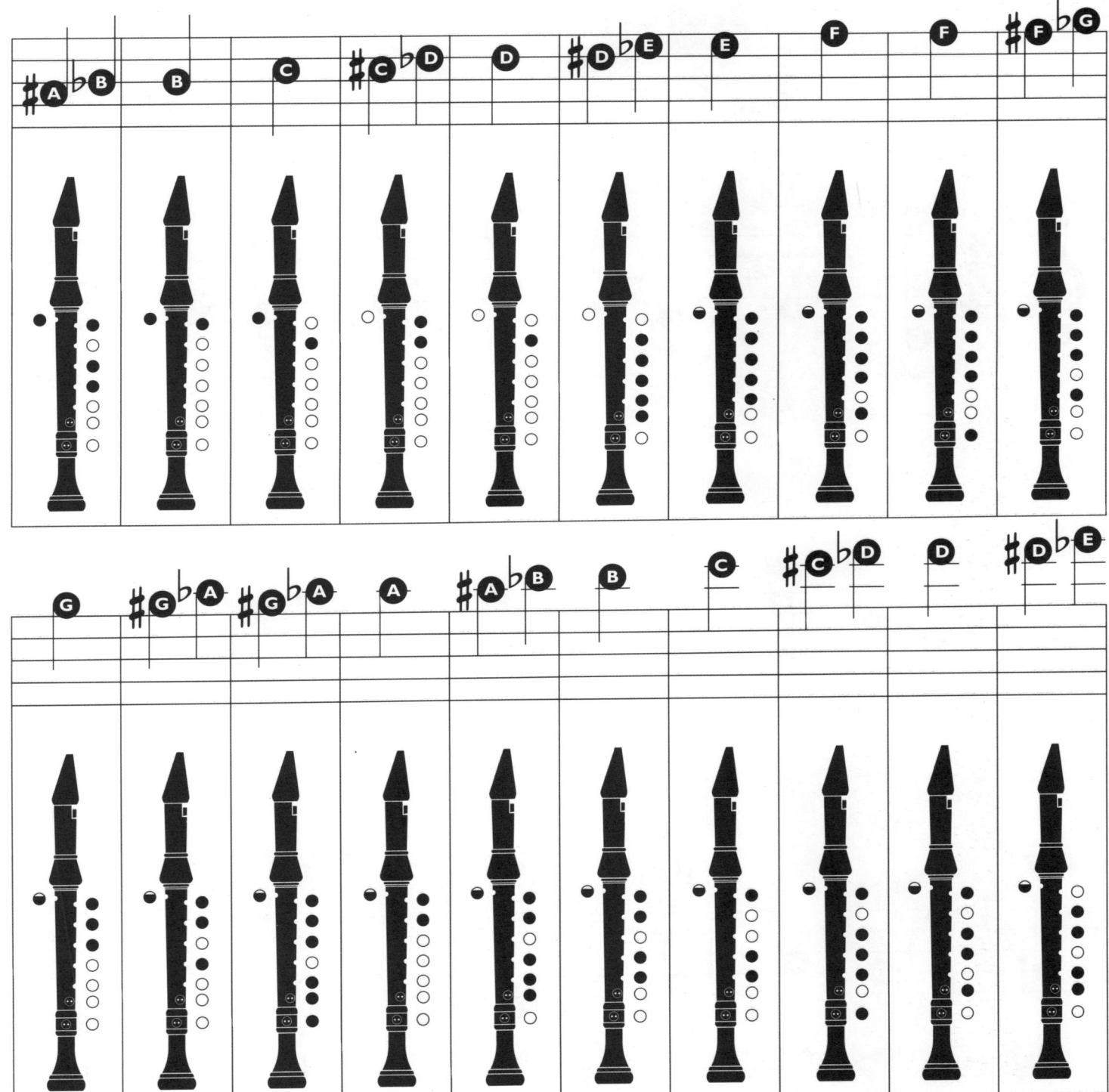

Auld Lang Syne

Traditional.

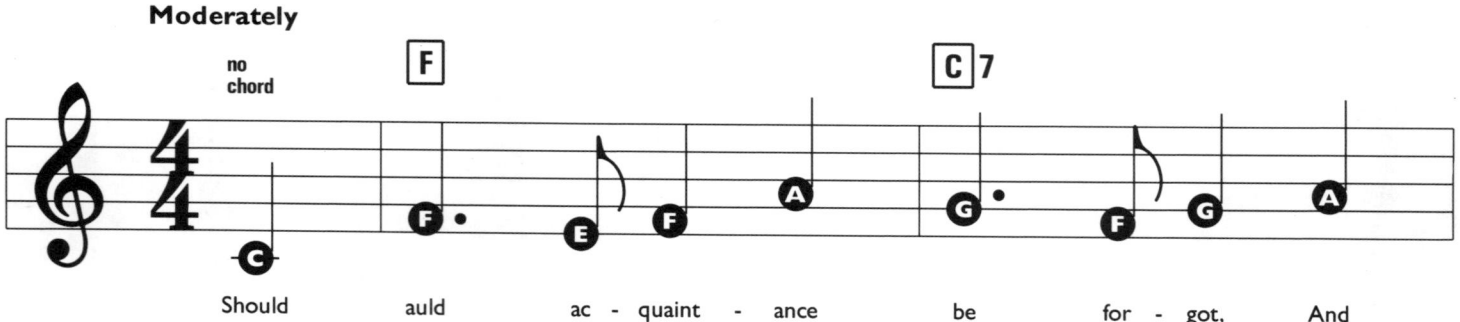

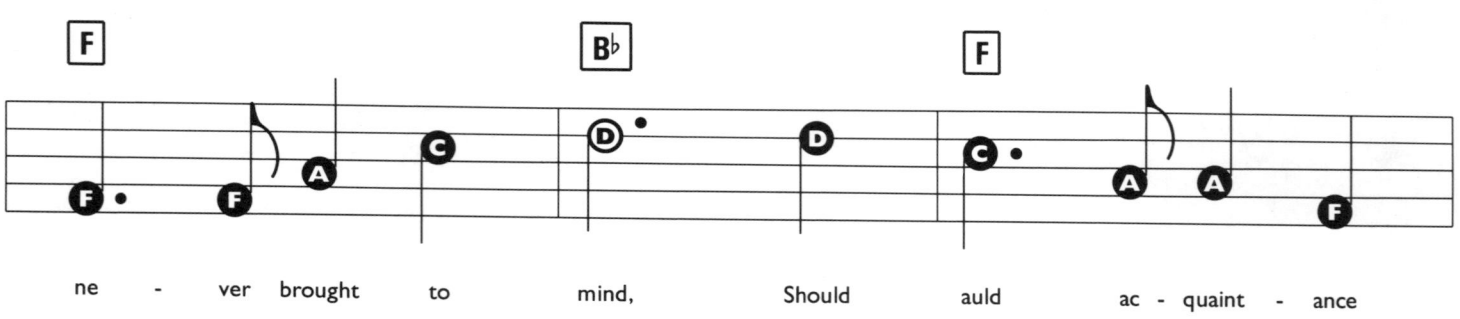

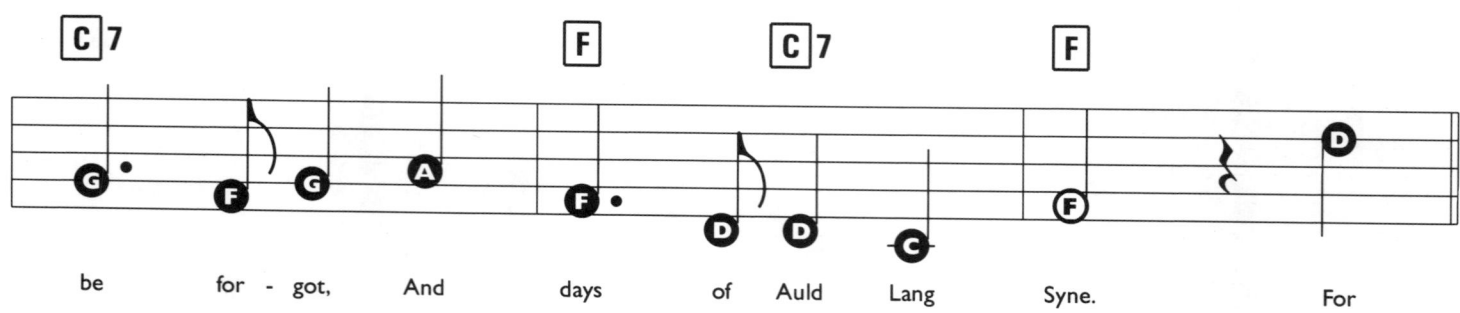

© Copyright 1993 Dorsey Brothers Music Limited, 8/9 Frith Street, London W1.
All Rights Reserved. International Copyright Secured.

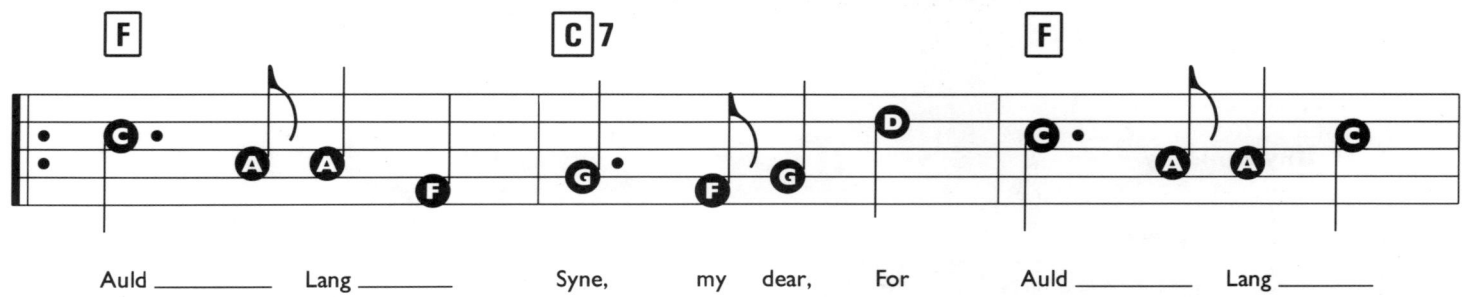
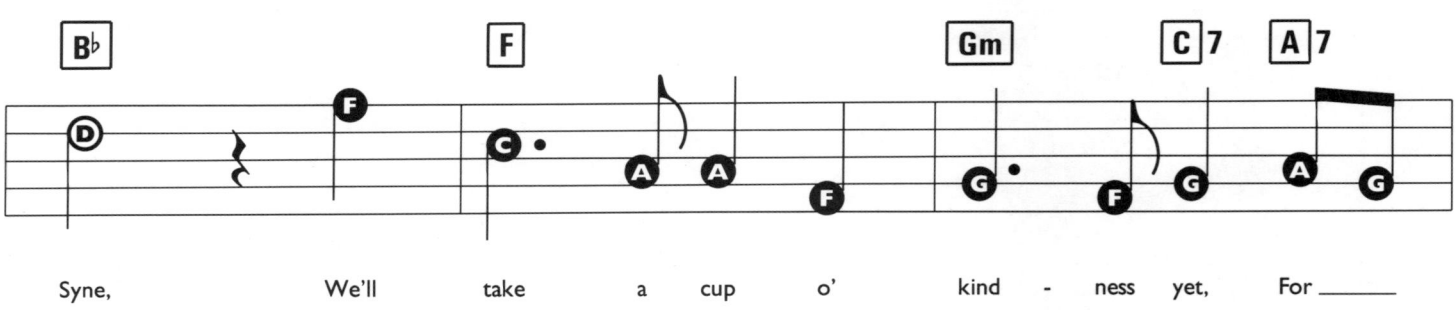
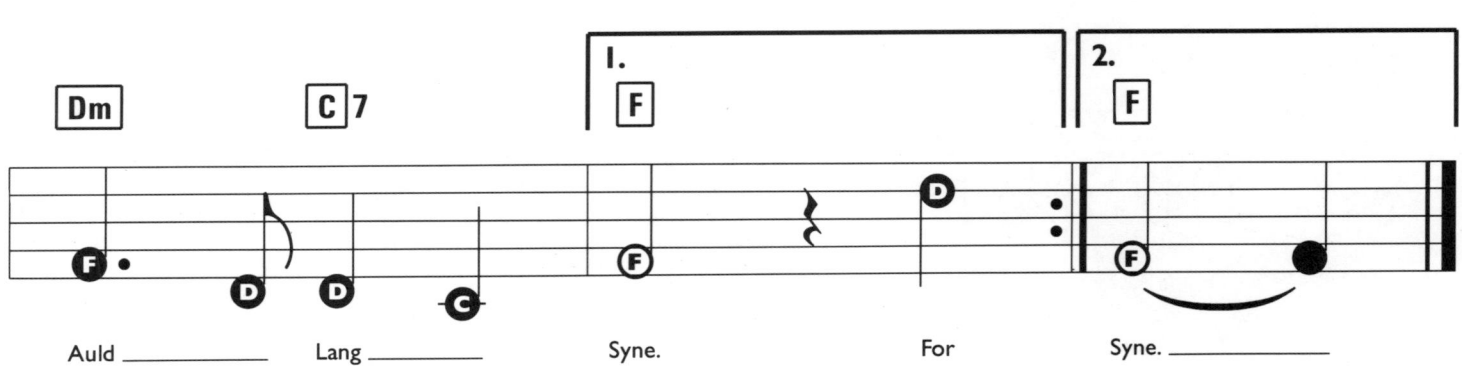

Blow The Man Down
Traditional.

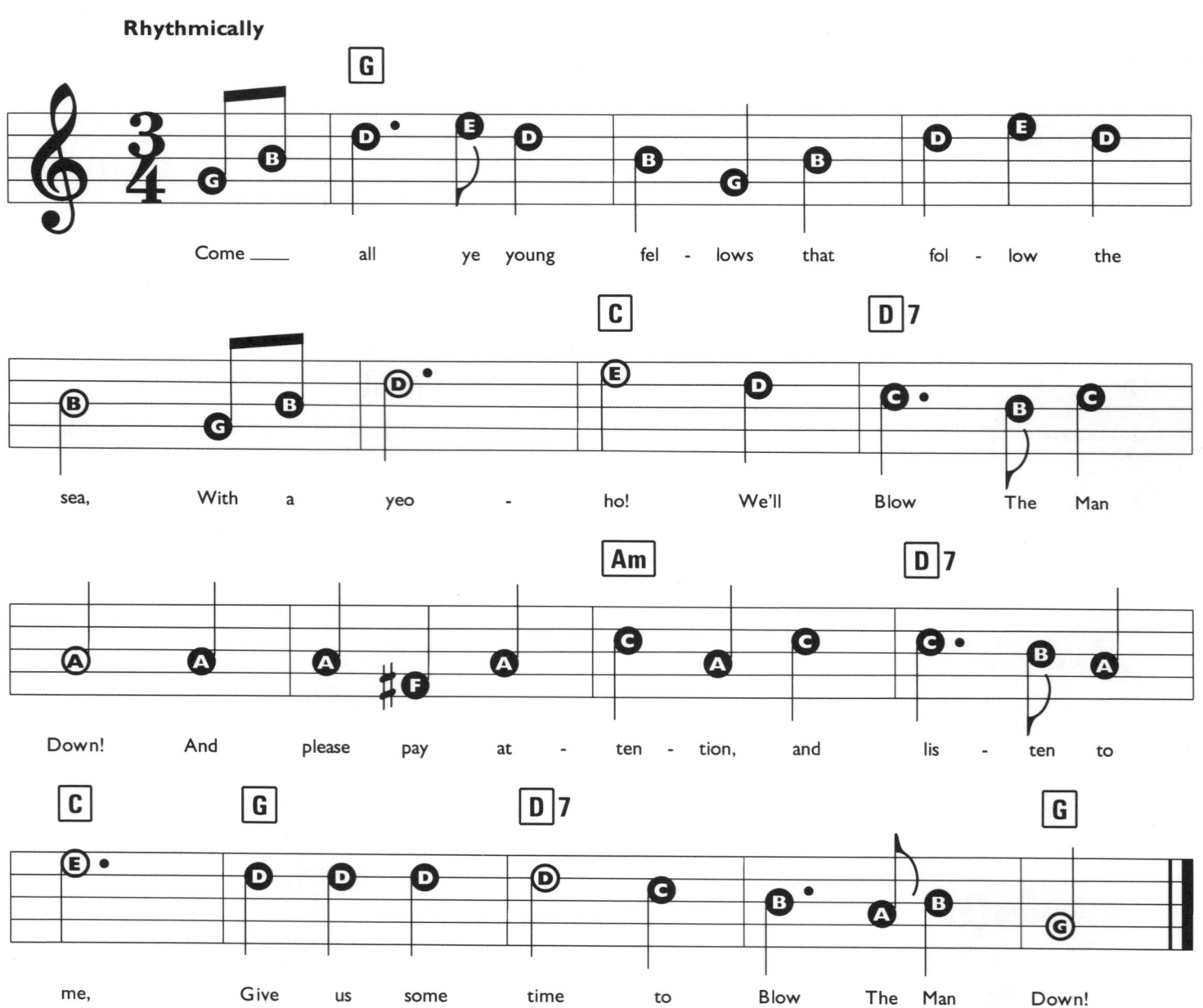

Early One Morning
Traditional.

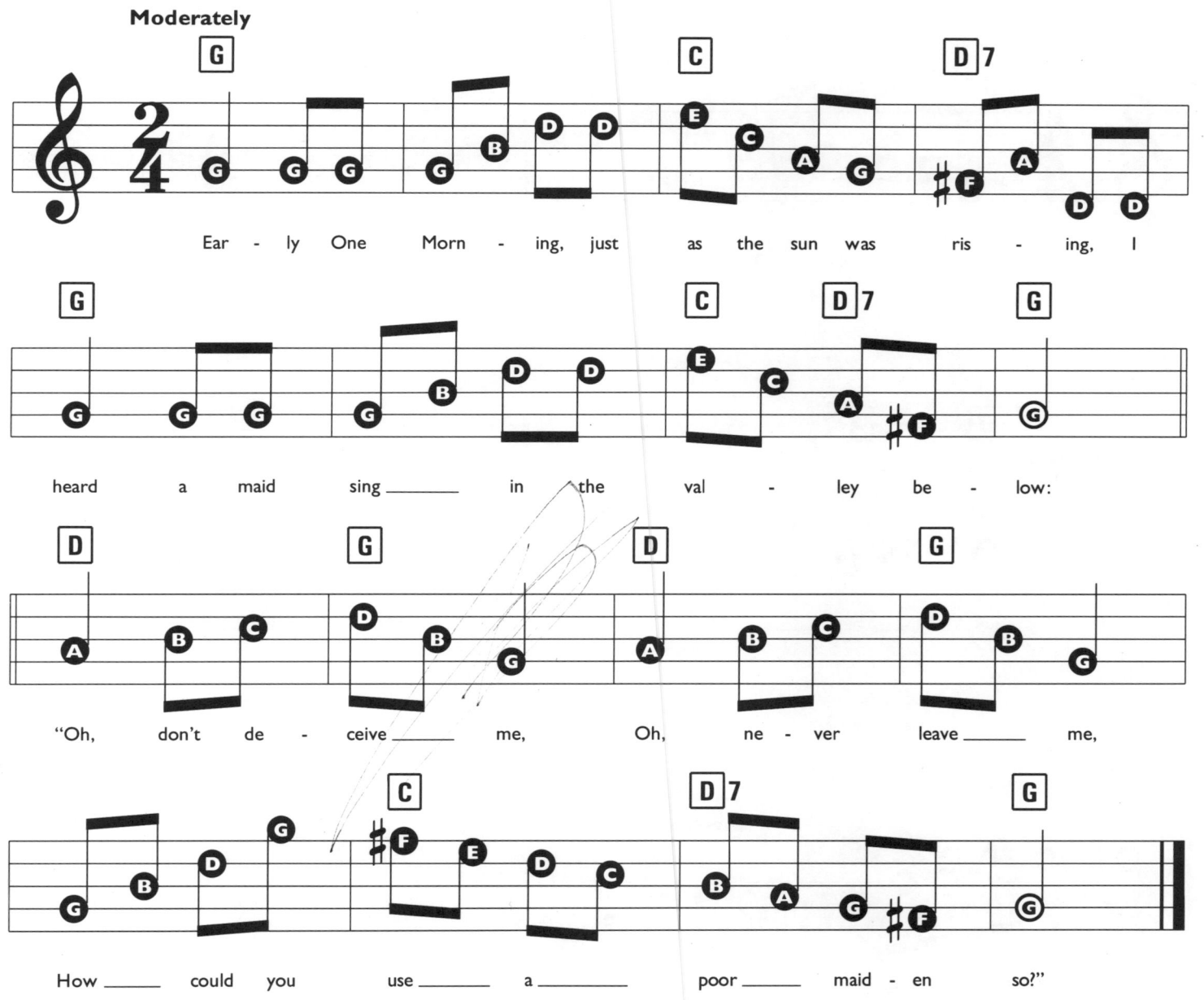

Cherry Ripe

Traditional.

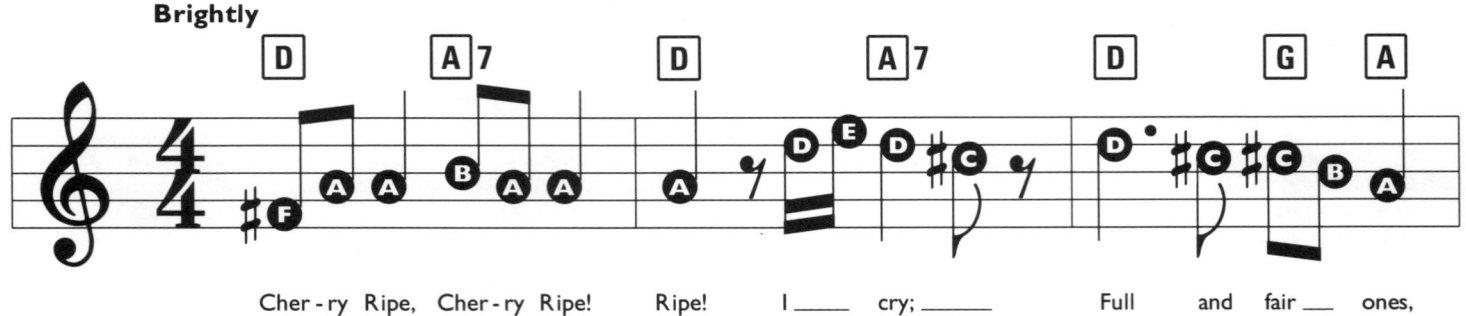
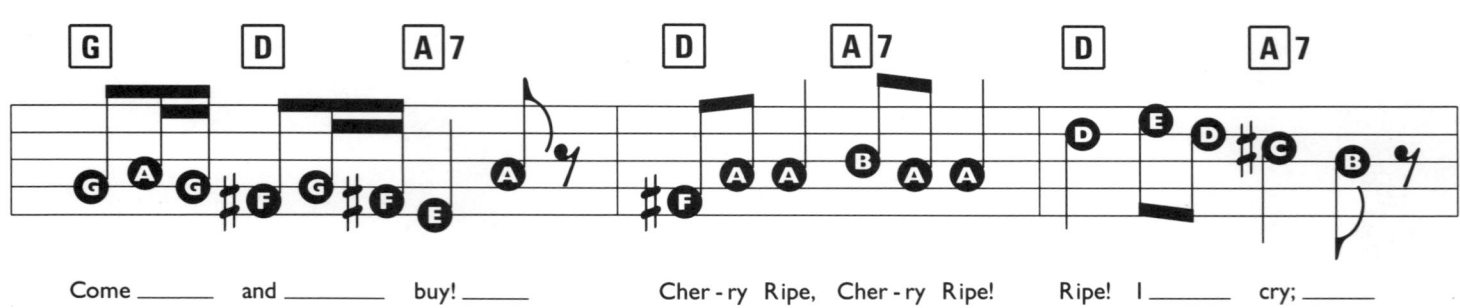
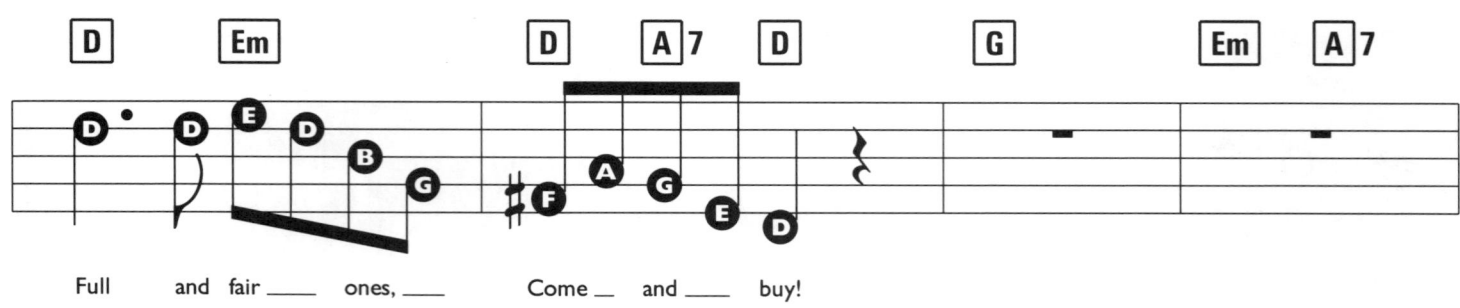

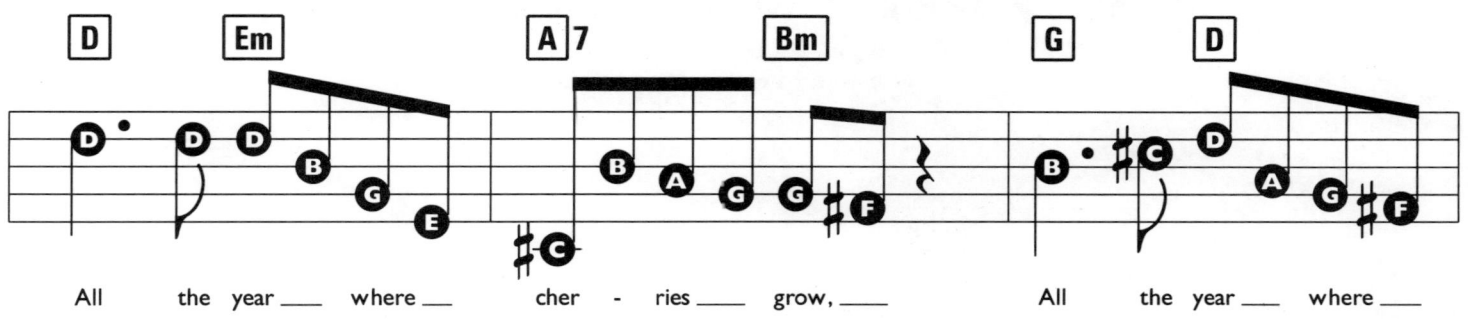
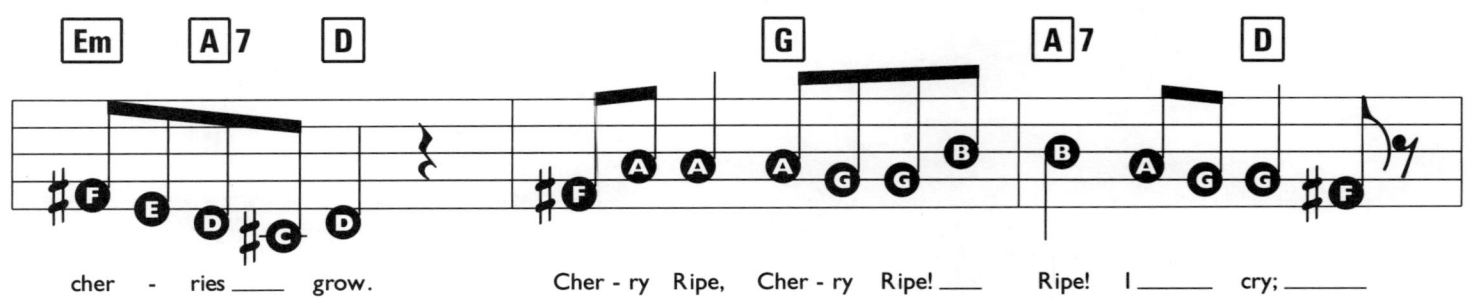
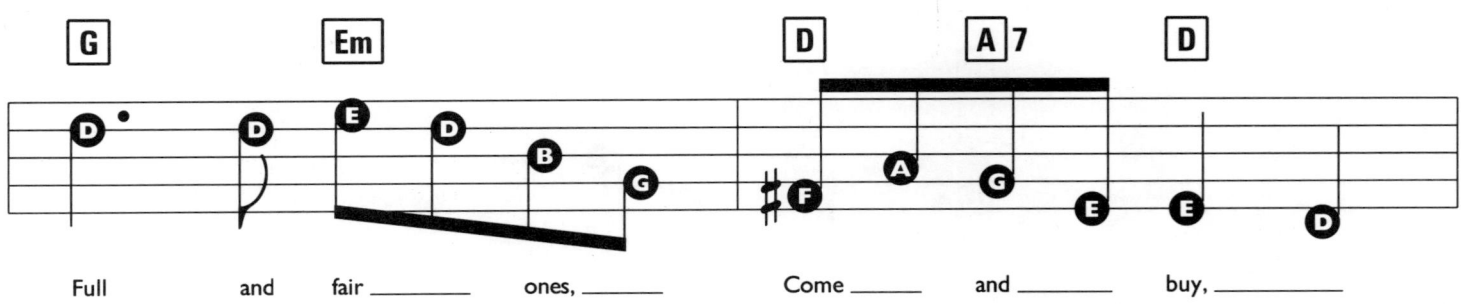
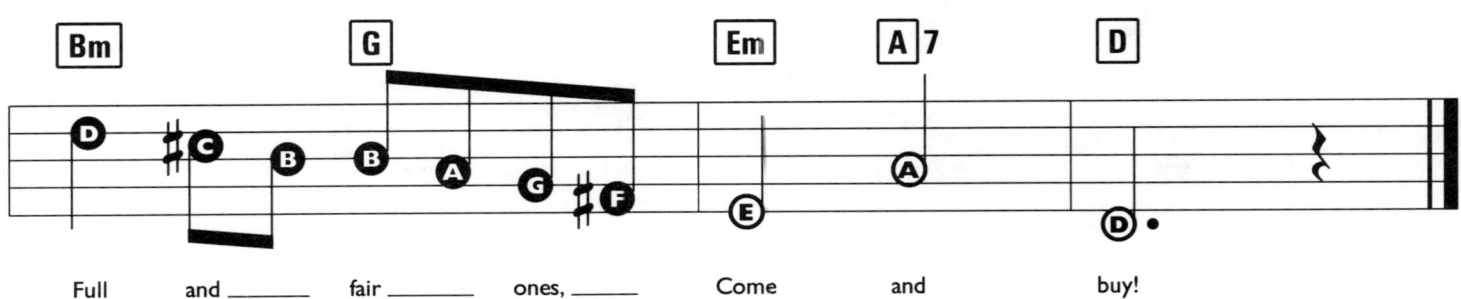

Danny Boy (Londonderry Air)

Traditional Irish Melody.
Words by Fred E. Weatherly.

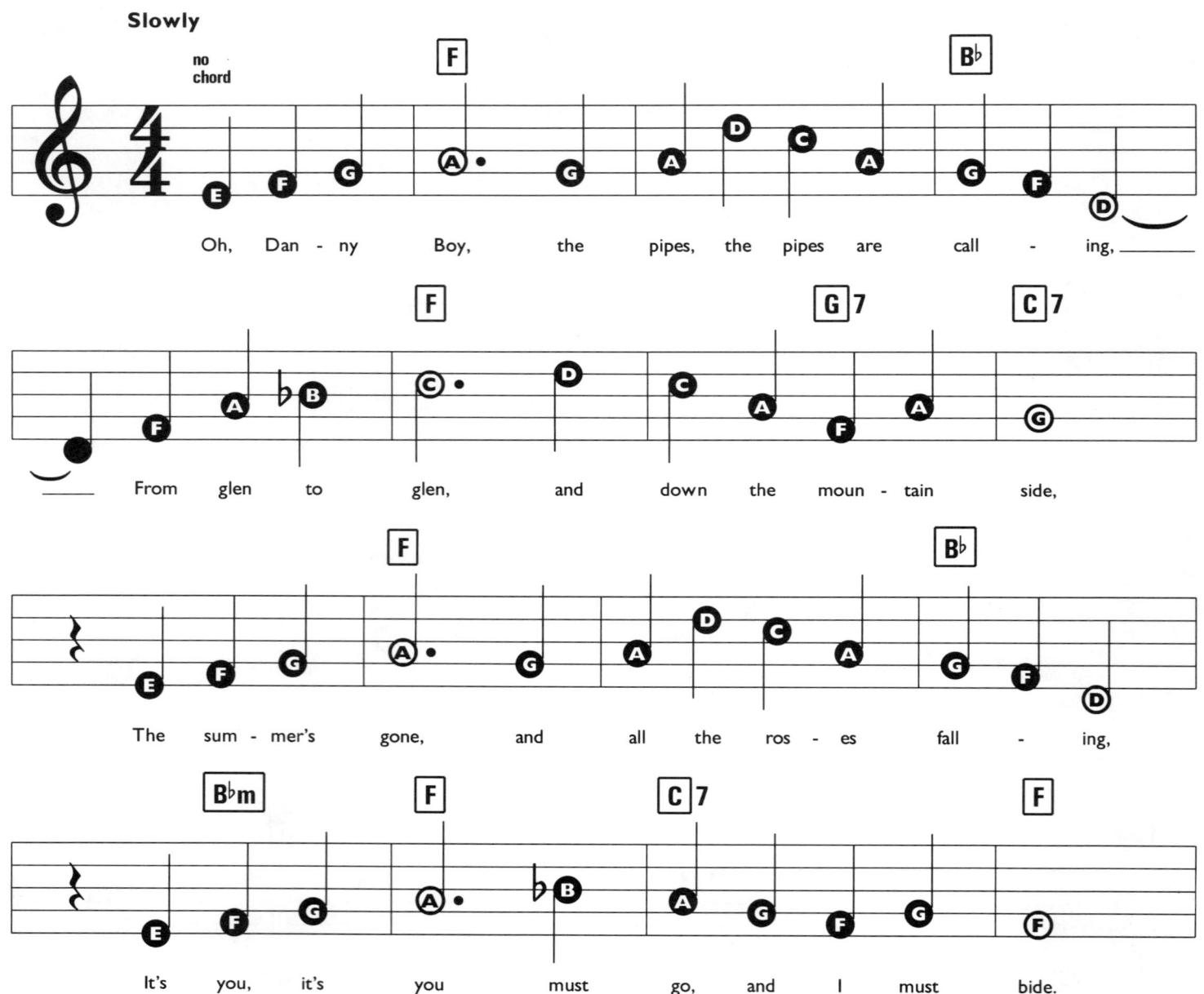

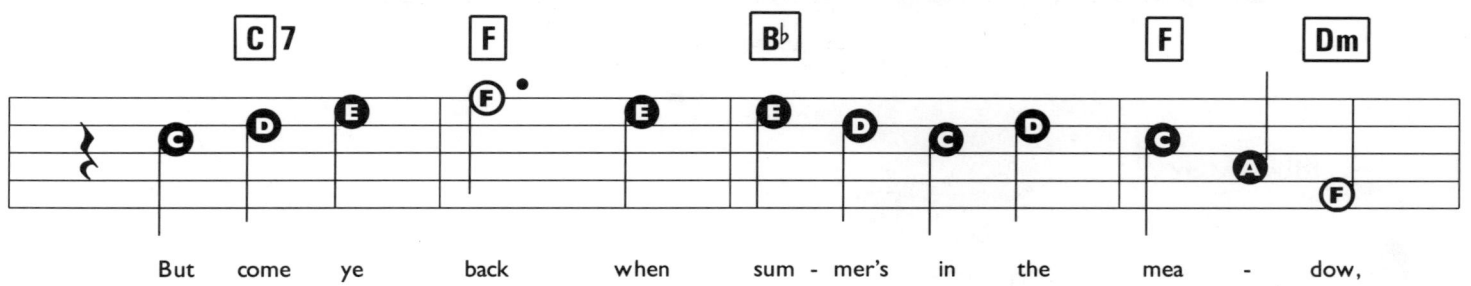
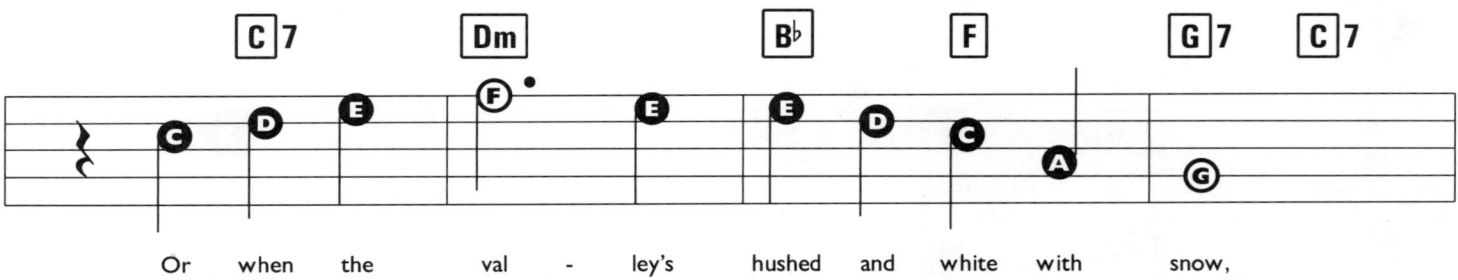
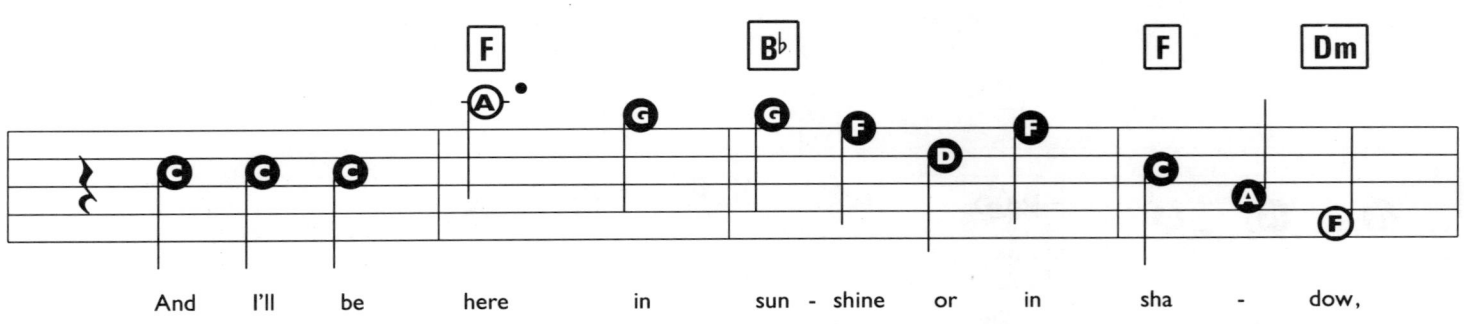
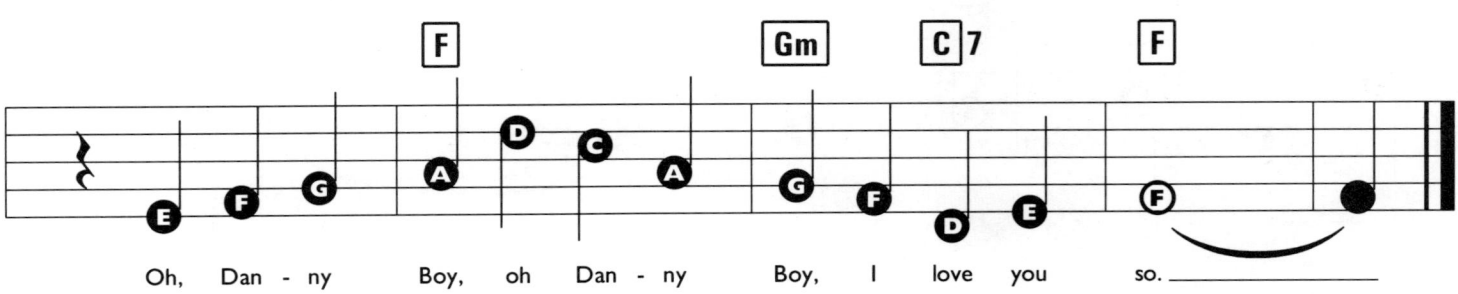

Drink To Me Only With Thine Eyes
Traditional.

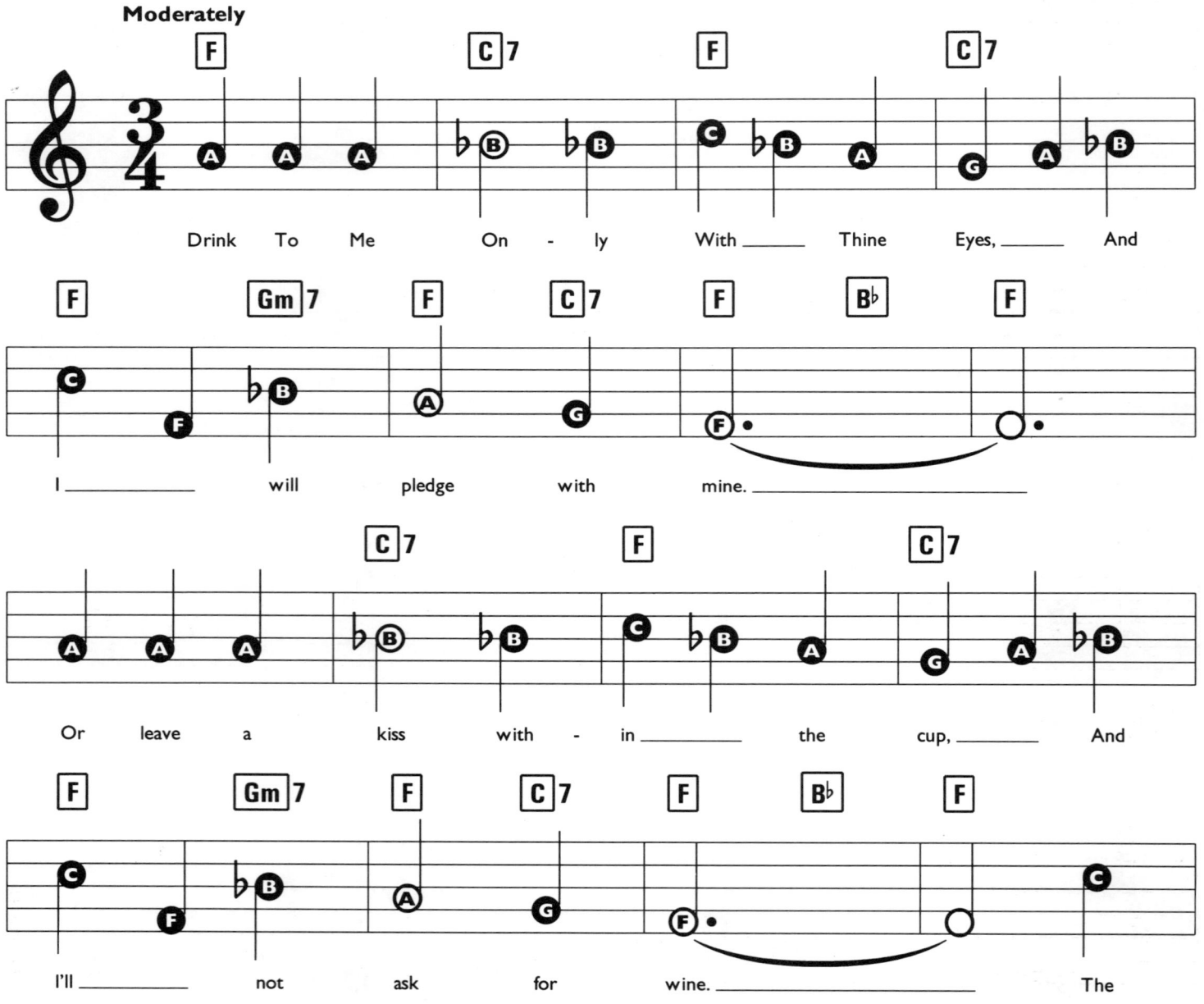

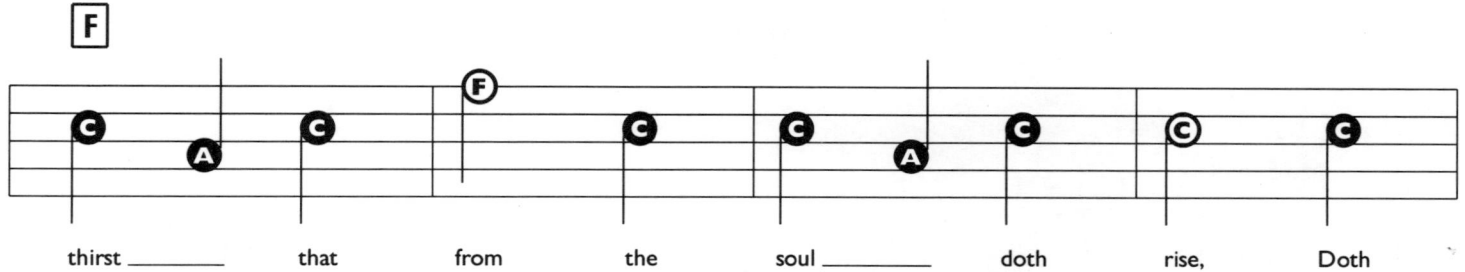
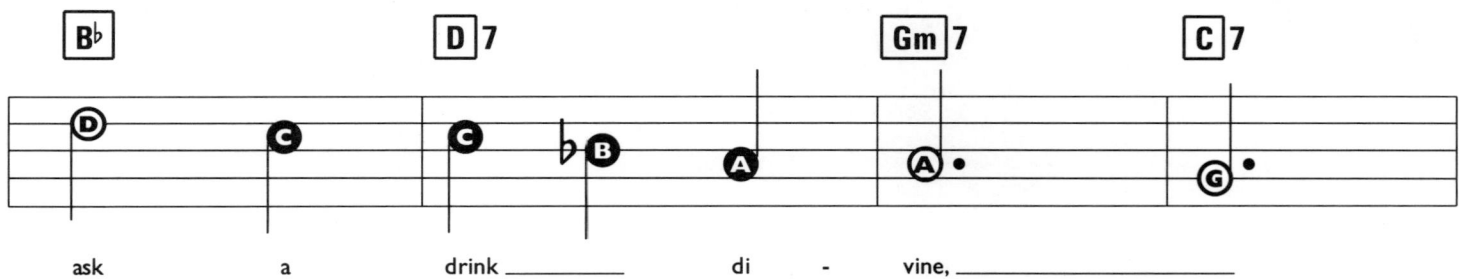
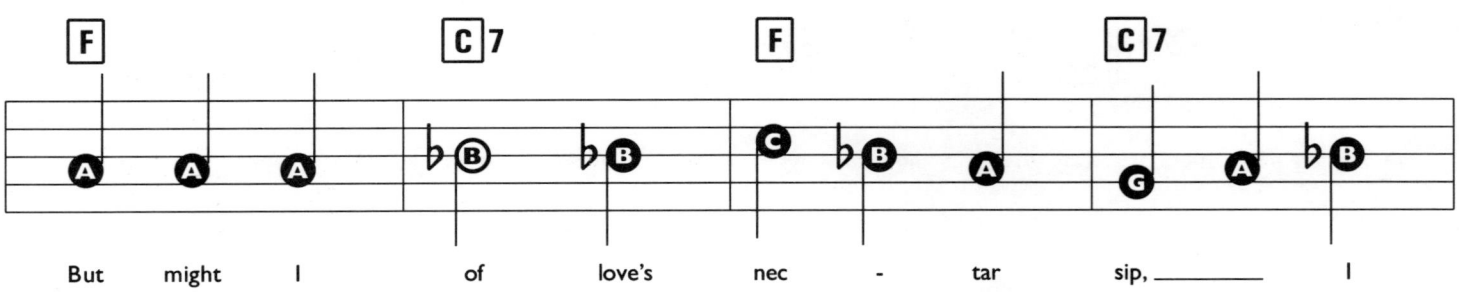
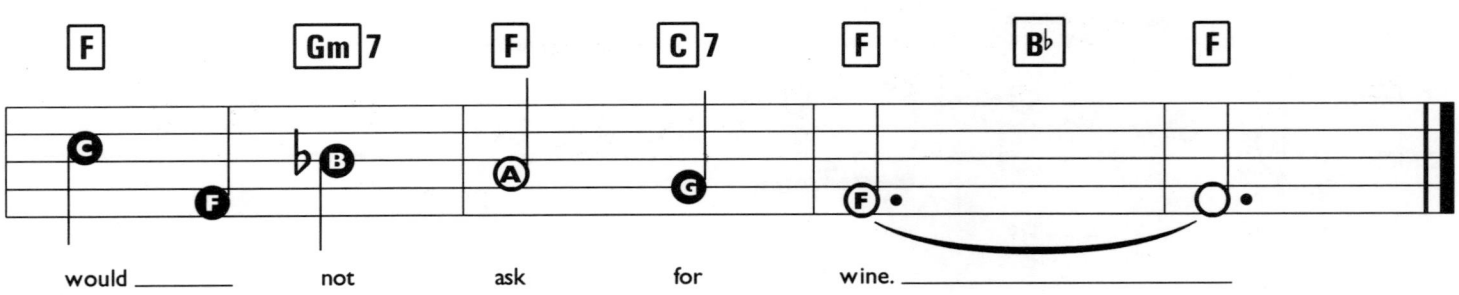

Greensleeves

Traditional.

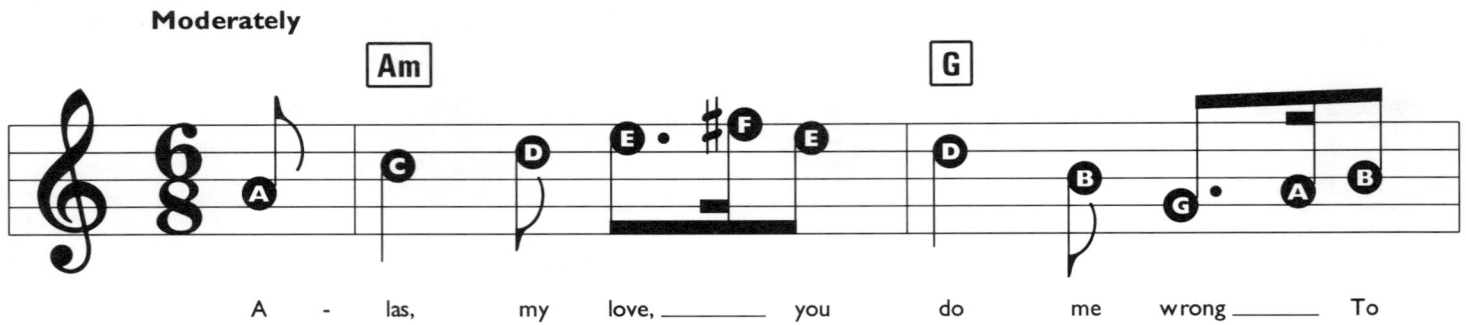

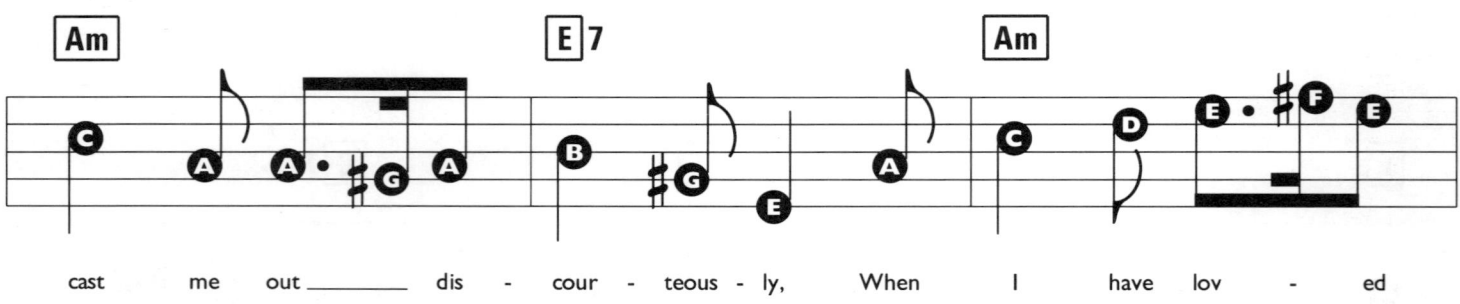

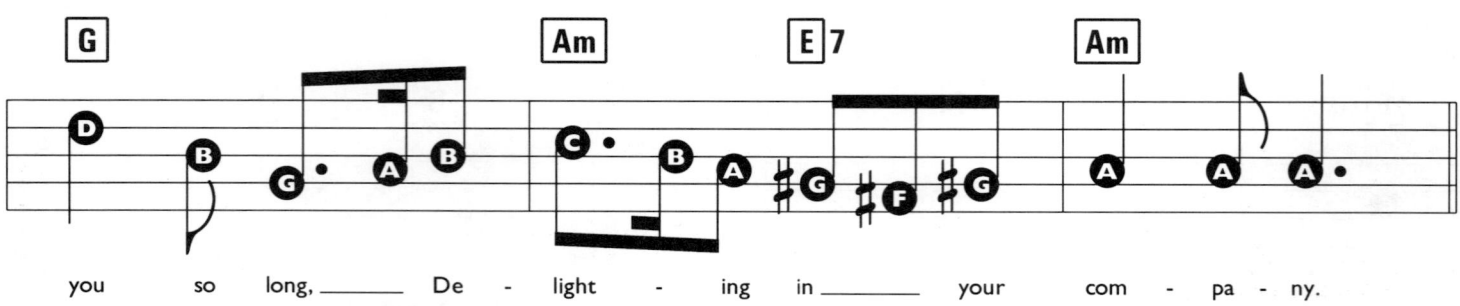

© Copyright 1993 Dorsey Brothers Music Limited, 8/9 Frith Street, London W1.
All Rights Reserved. International Copyright Secured.

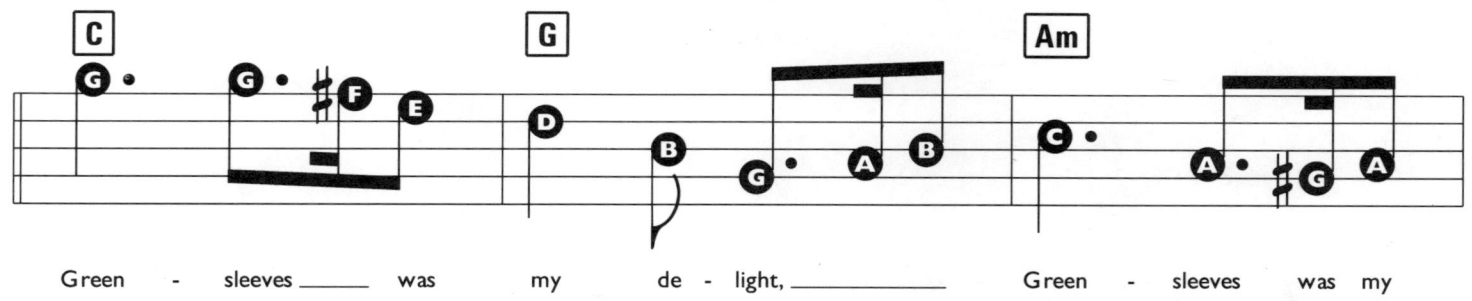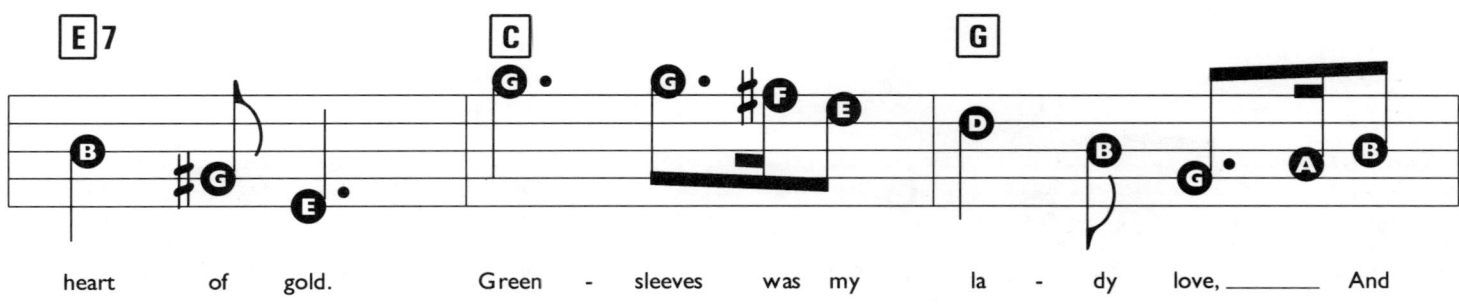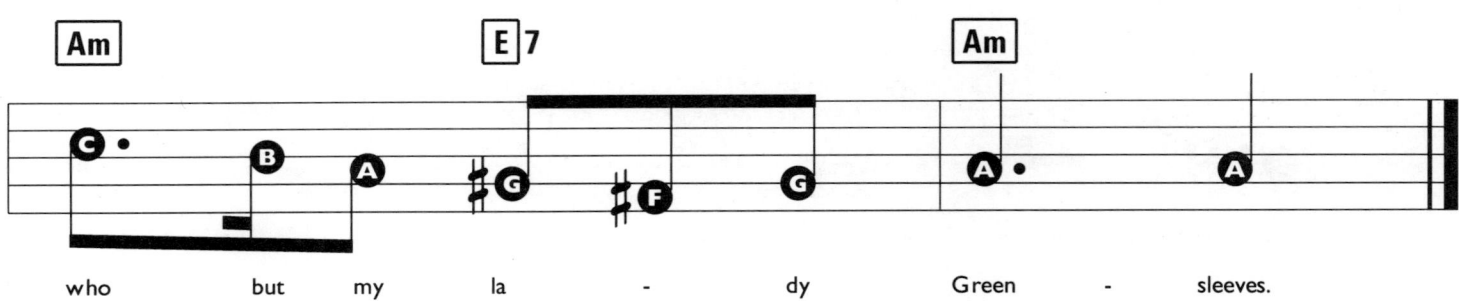

Hearts Of Oak
Traditional.

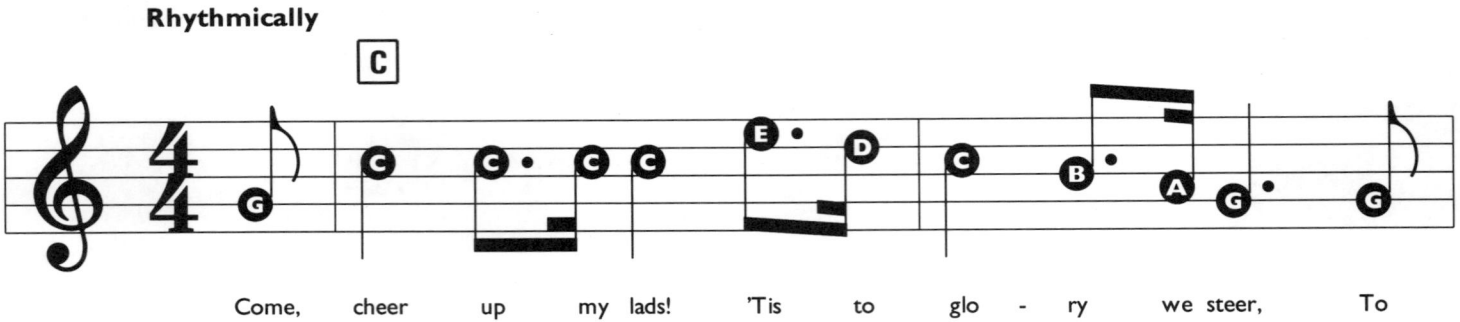
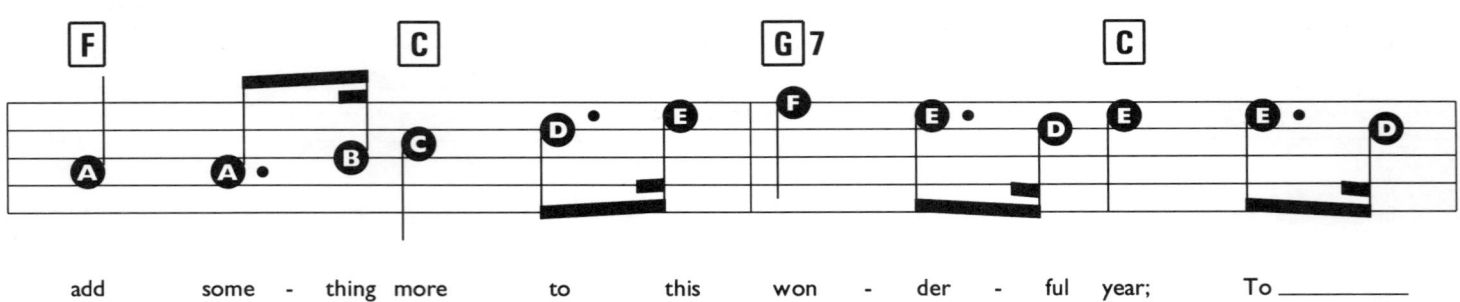
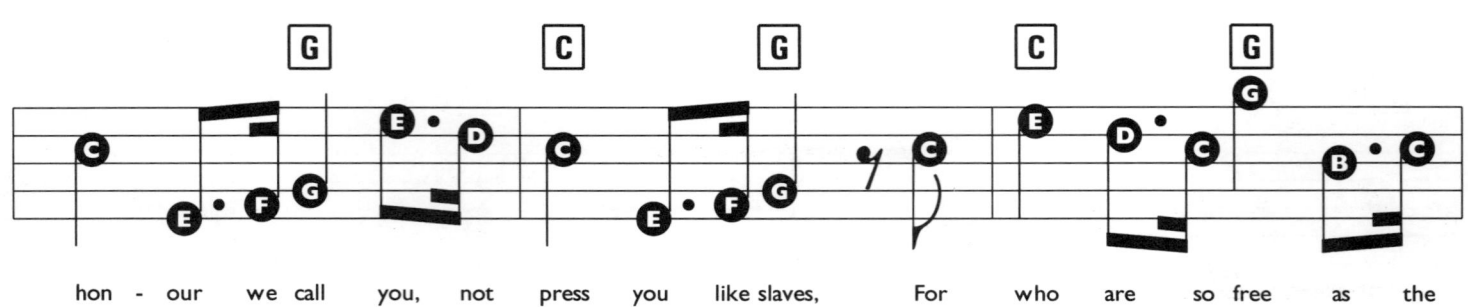

© Copyright 1993 Dorsey Brothers Music Limited, 8/9 Frith Street, London W1.
All Rights Reserved. International Copyright Secured.

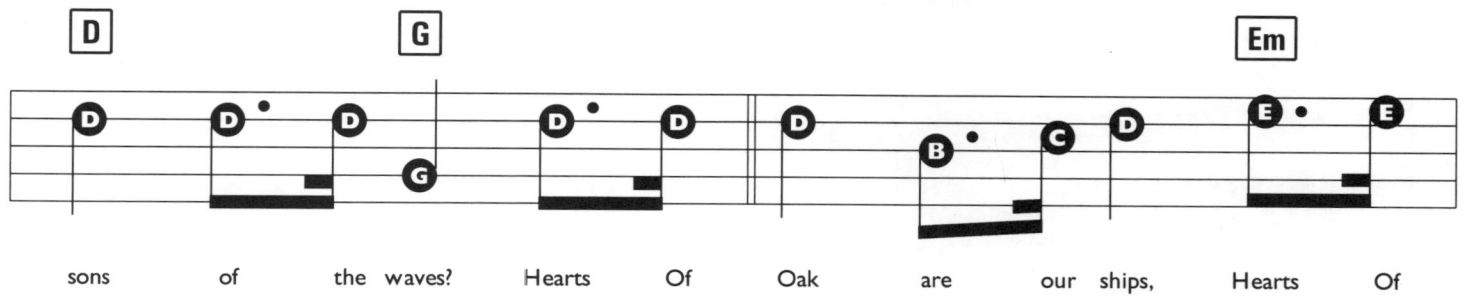
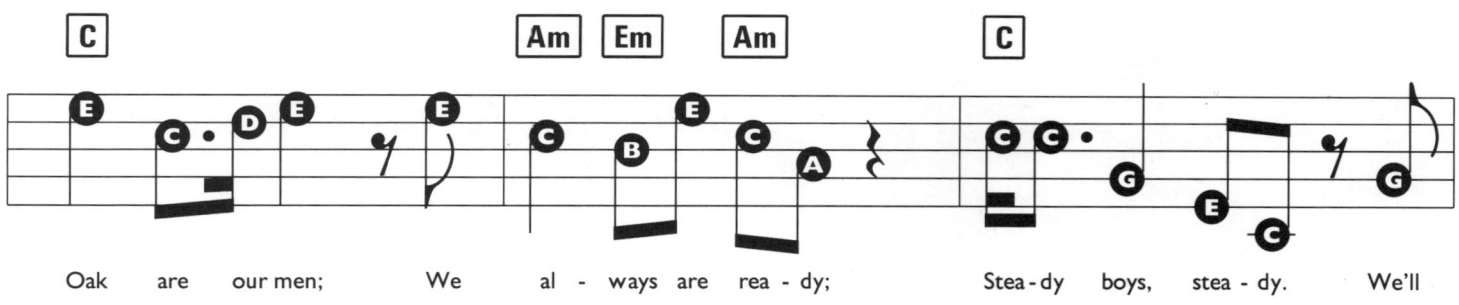
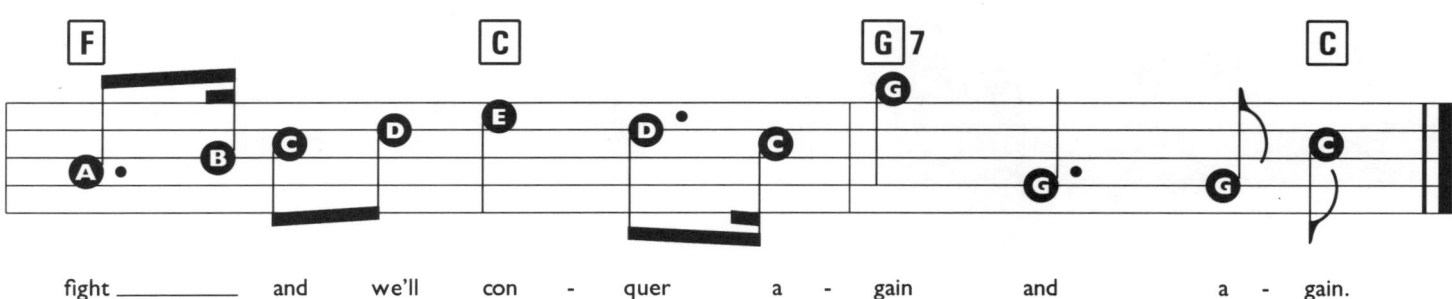

Home Sweet Home

Traditional.

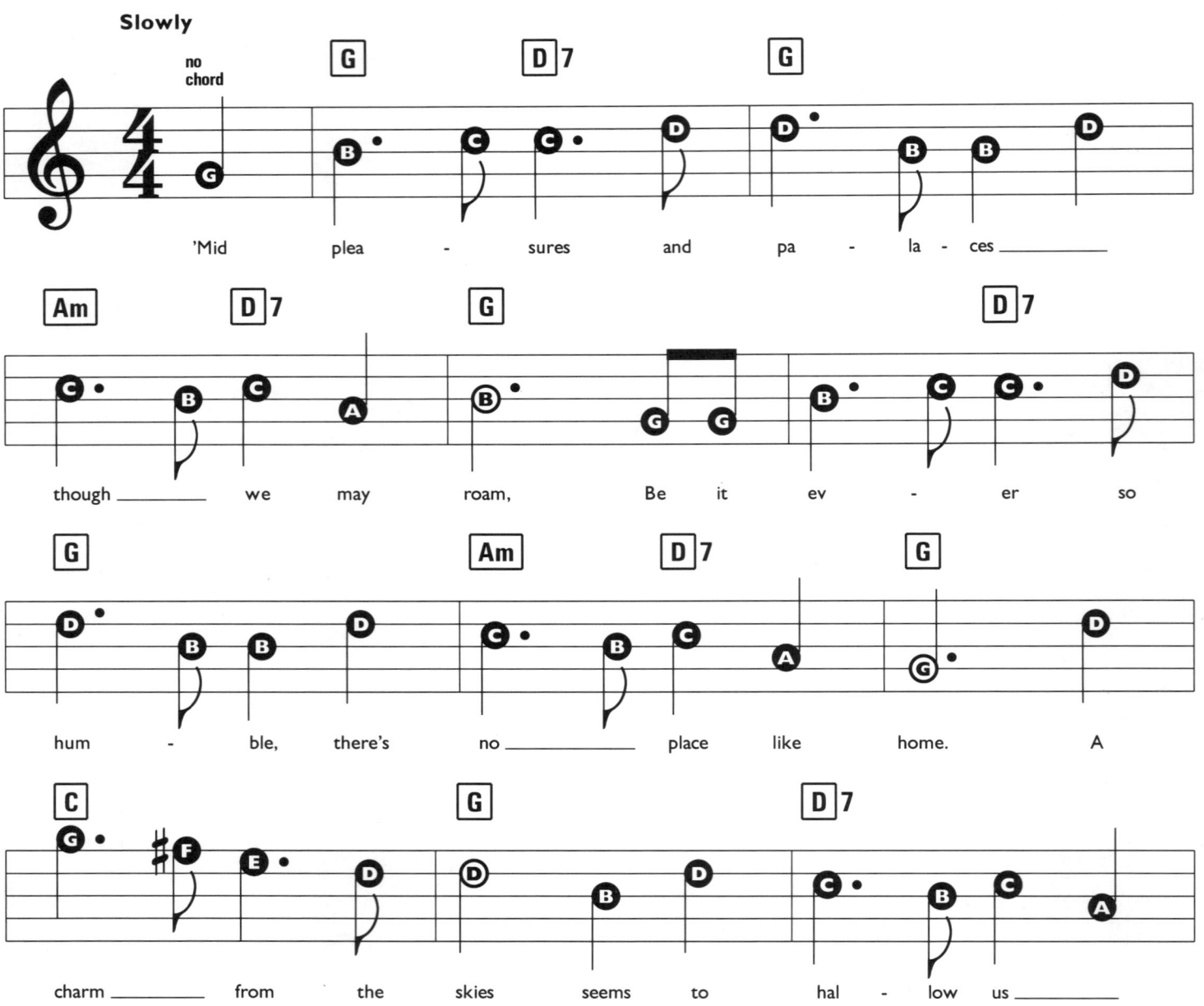

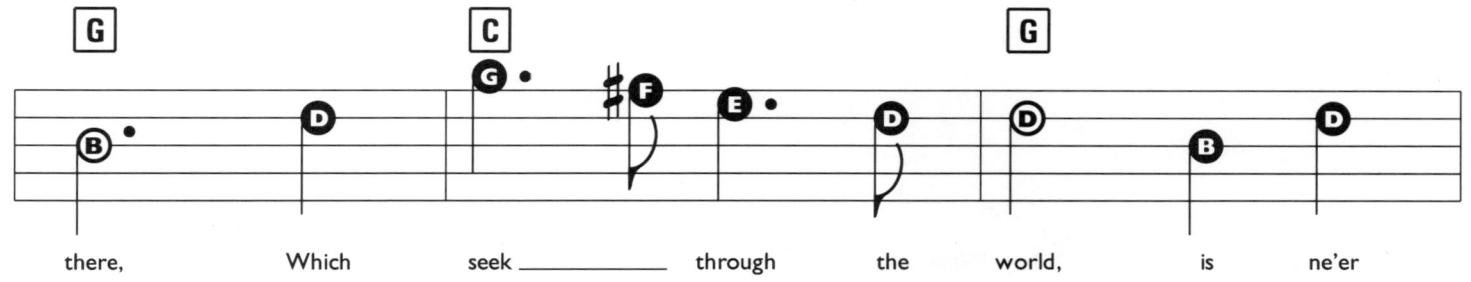
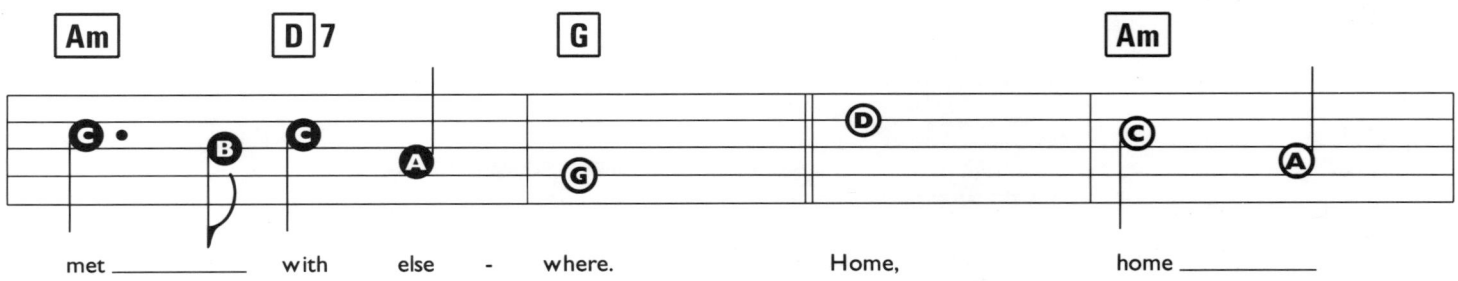
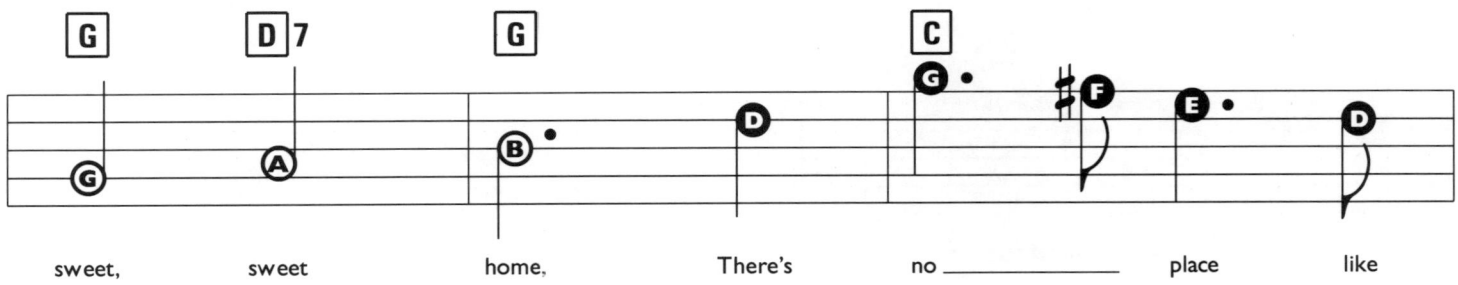
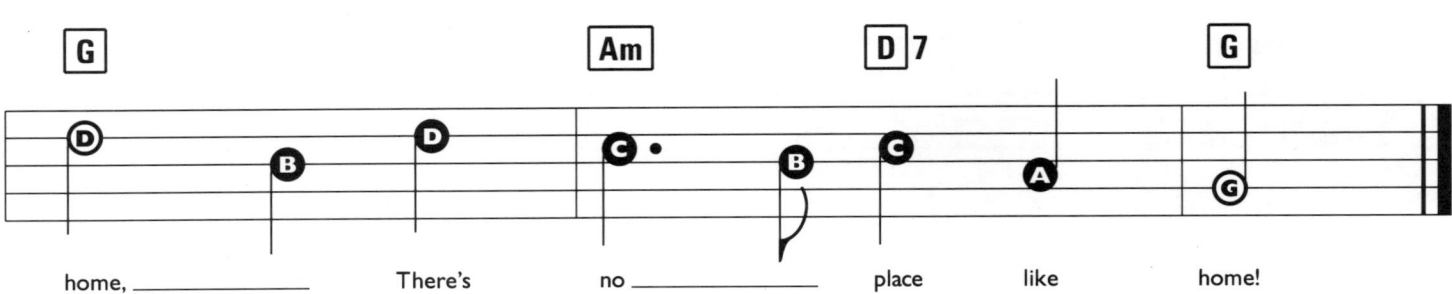

On Ilkley Moor Baht'at
Traditional.

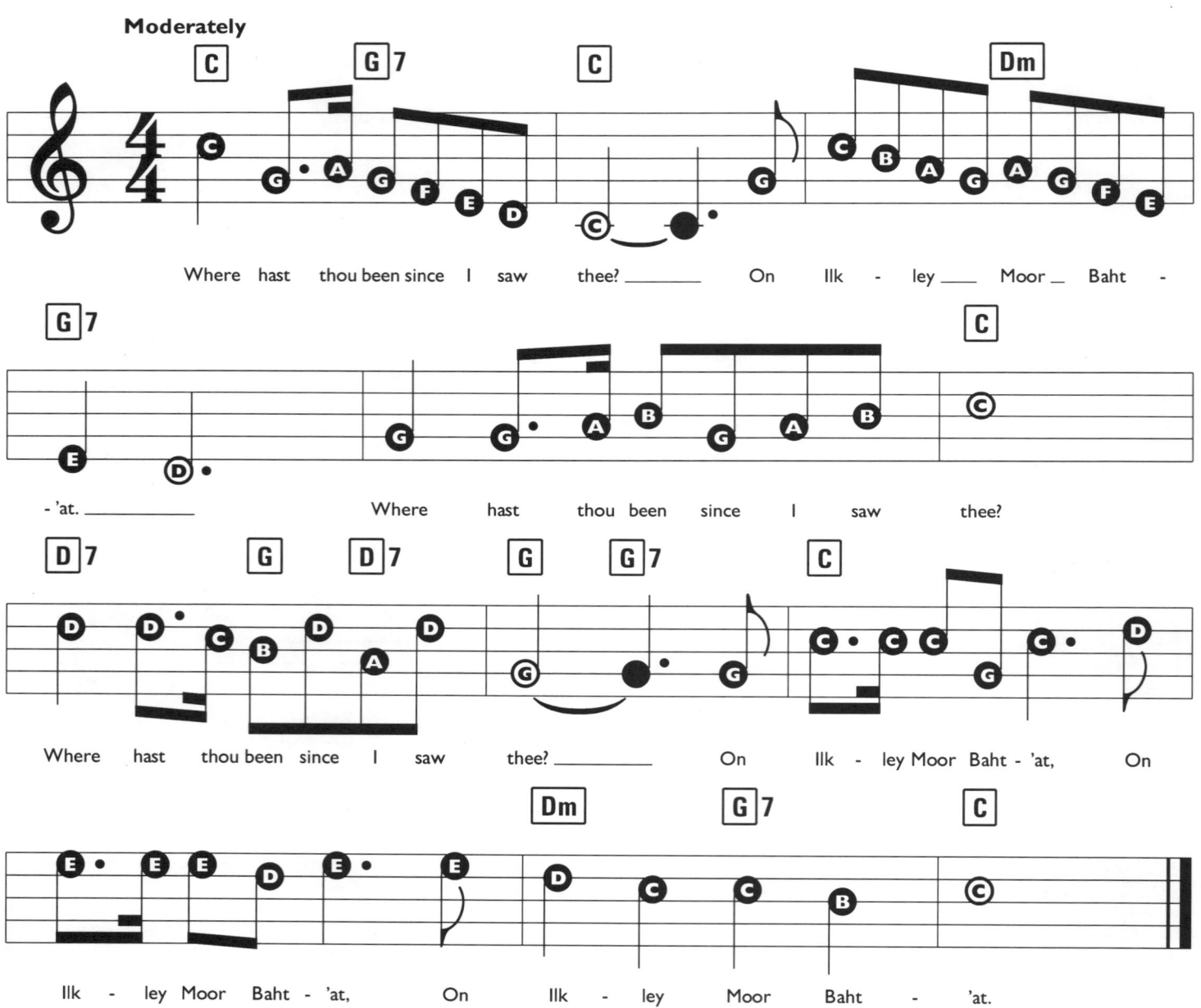

Scarborough Fair
Traditional.

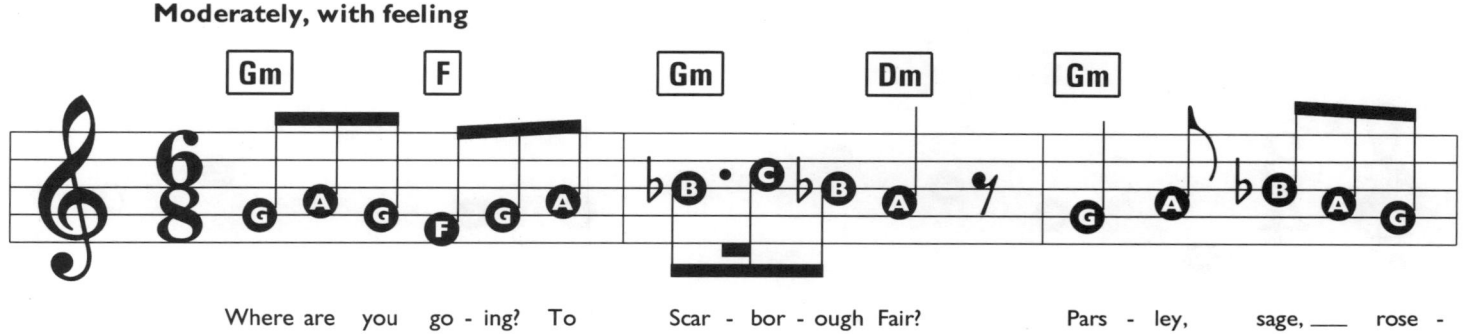
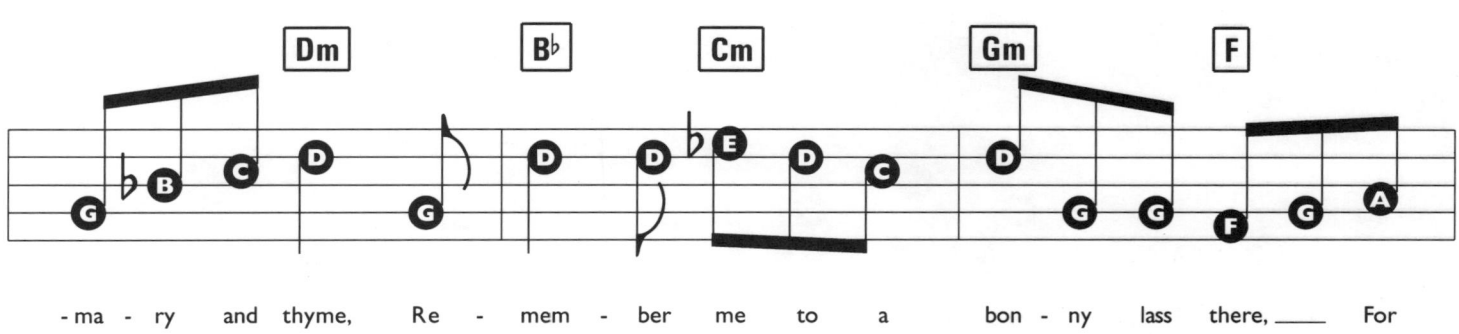
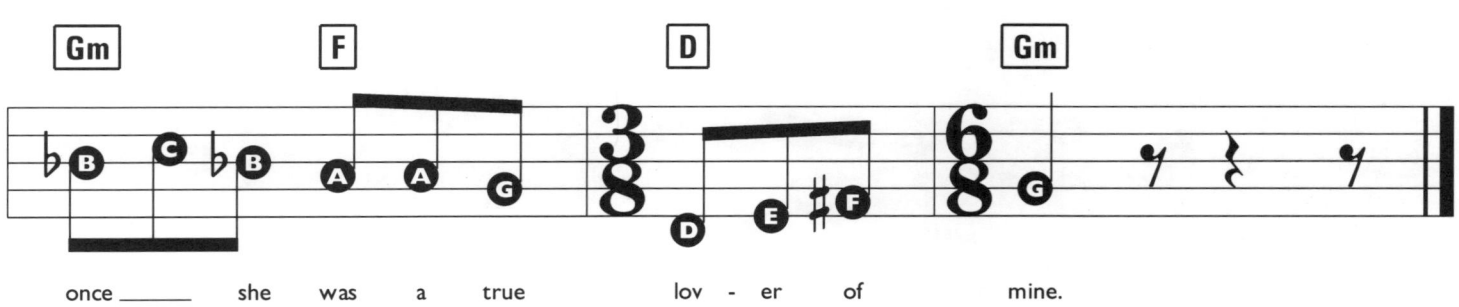

© Copyright 1993 Dorsey Brothers Music Limited, 8/9 Frith Street, London W1.
All Rights Reserved. International Copyright Secured.

The Ash Grove

Traditional.

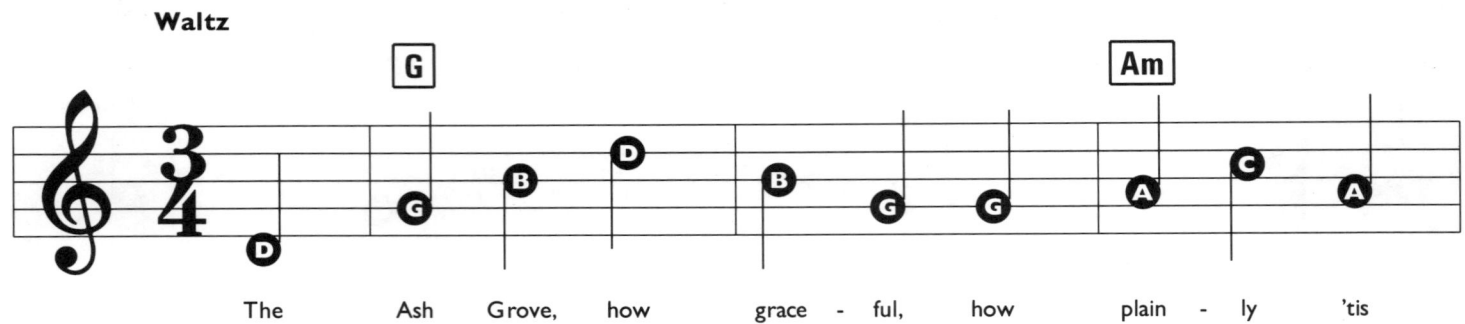
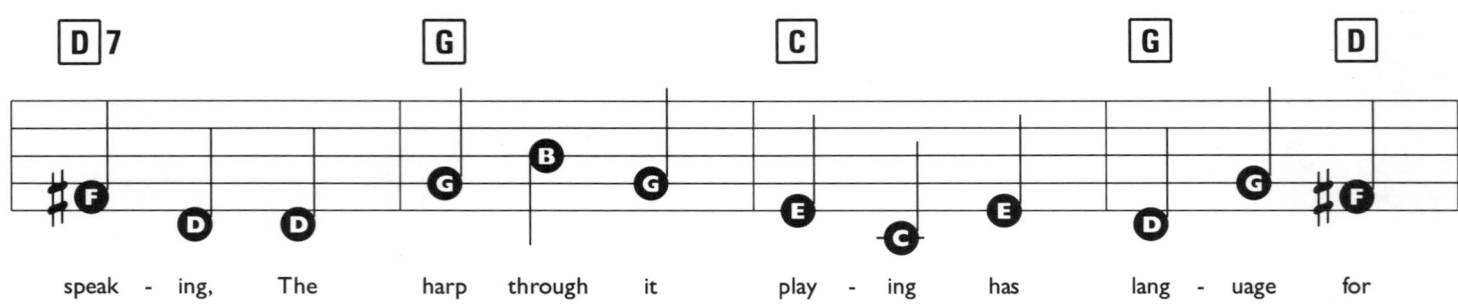
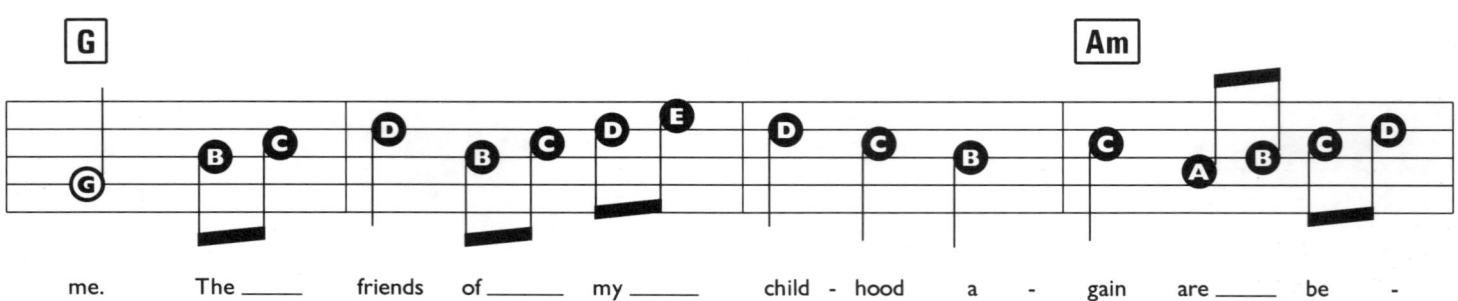

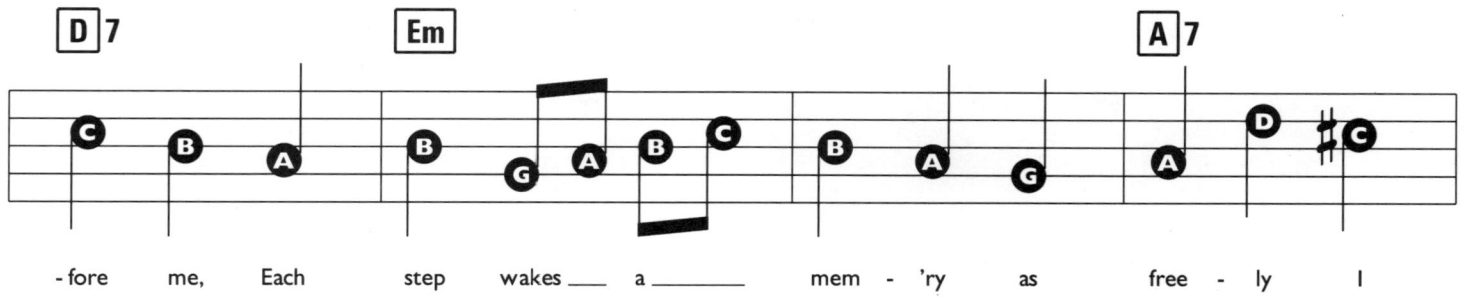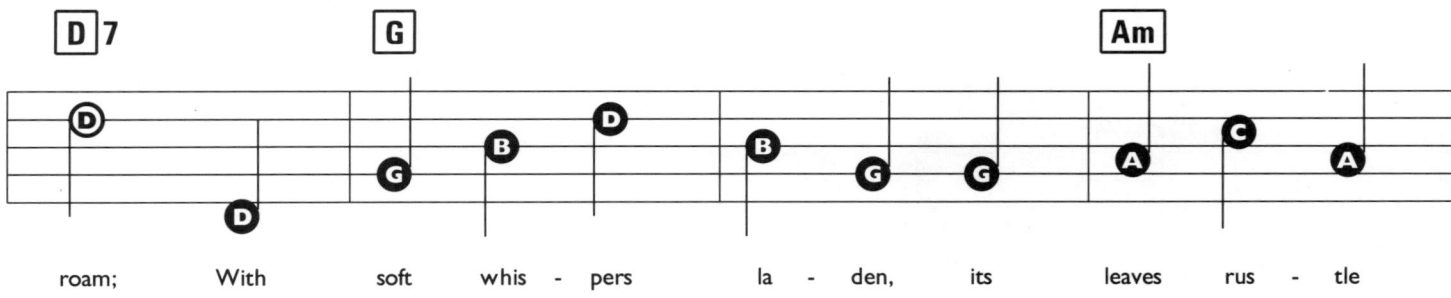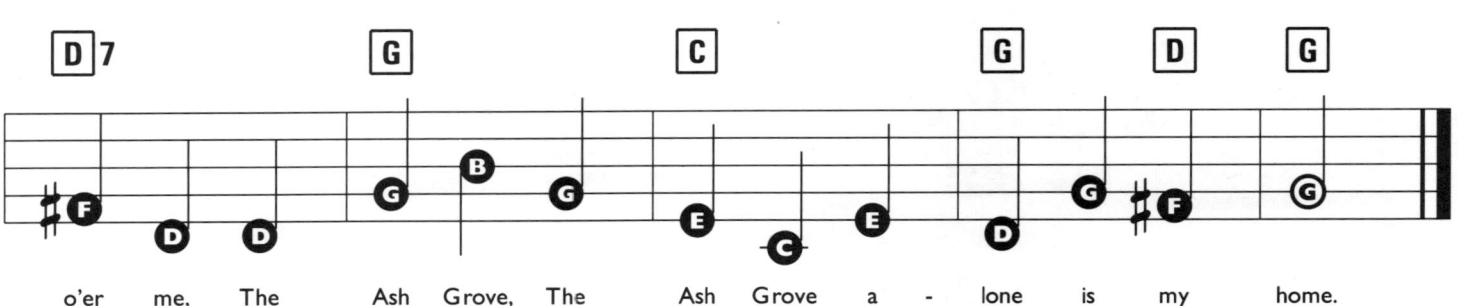

The Vicar Of Bray

Traditional.

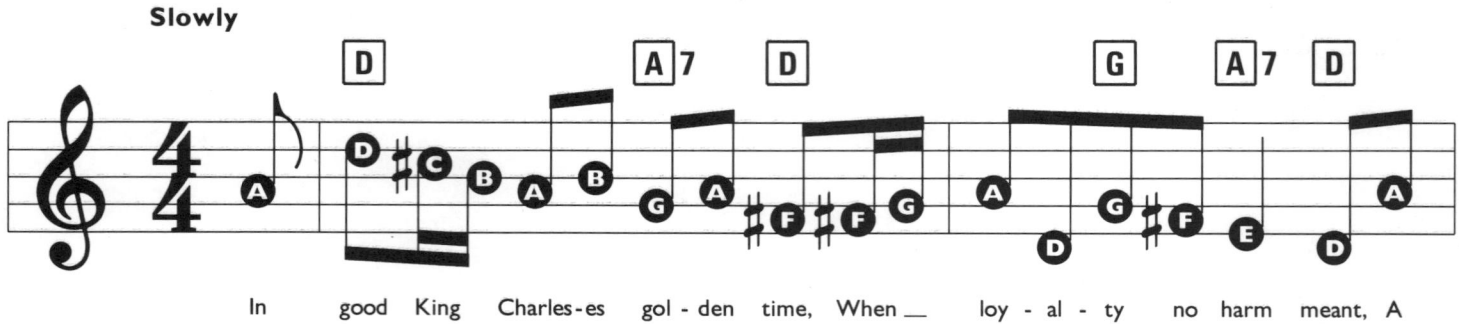

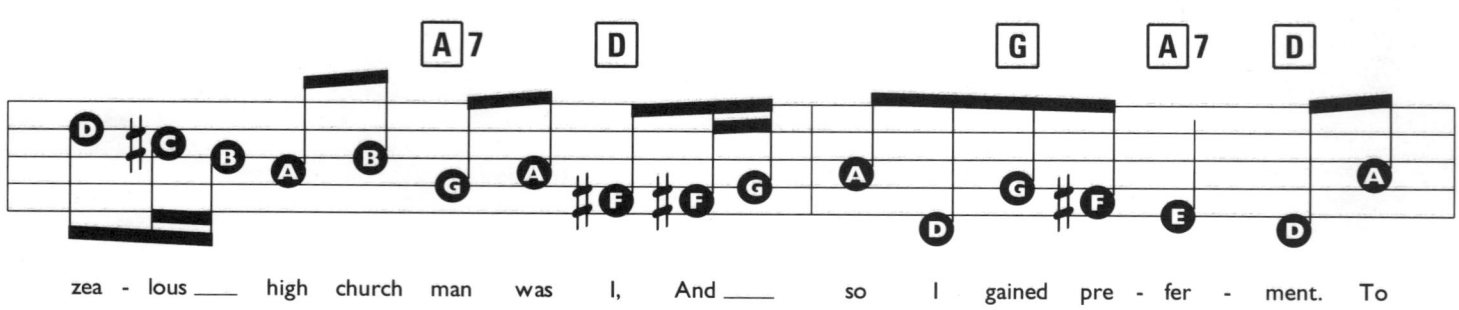

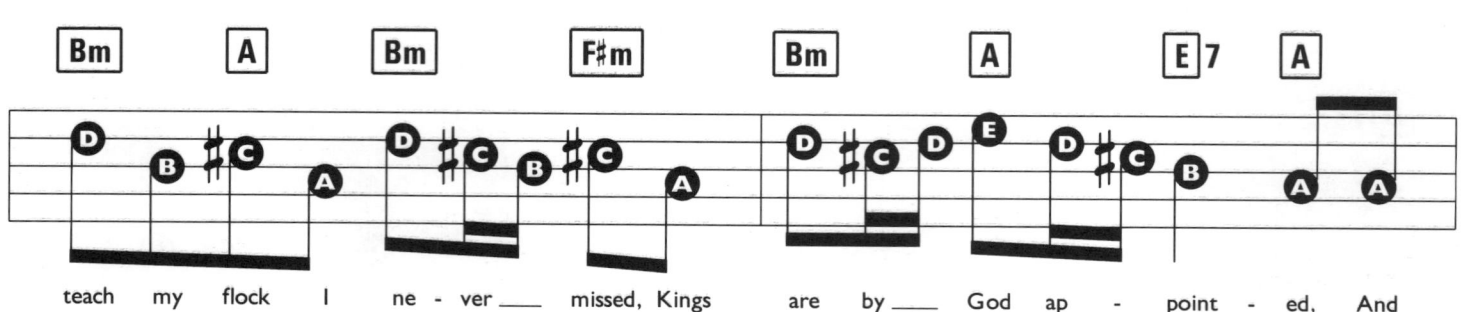

© Copyright 1993 Dorsey Brothers Music Limited, 8/9 Frith Street, London W1.
All Rights Reserved. International Copyright Secured.

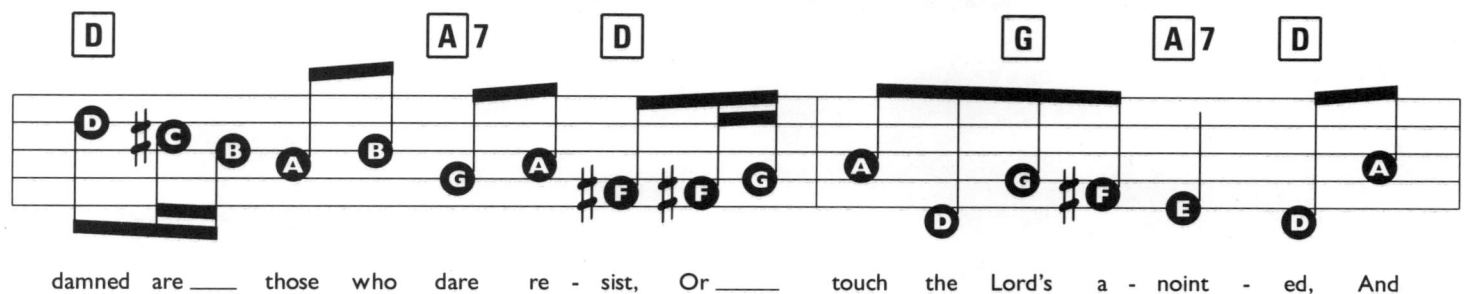
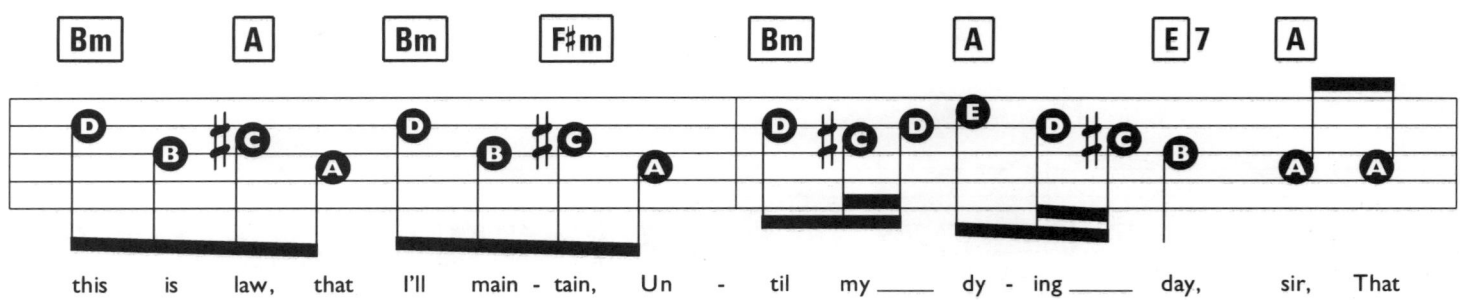
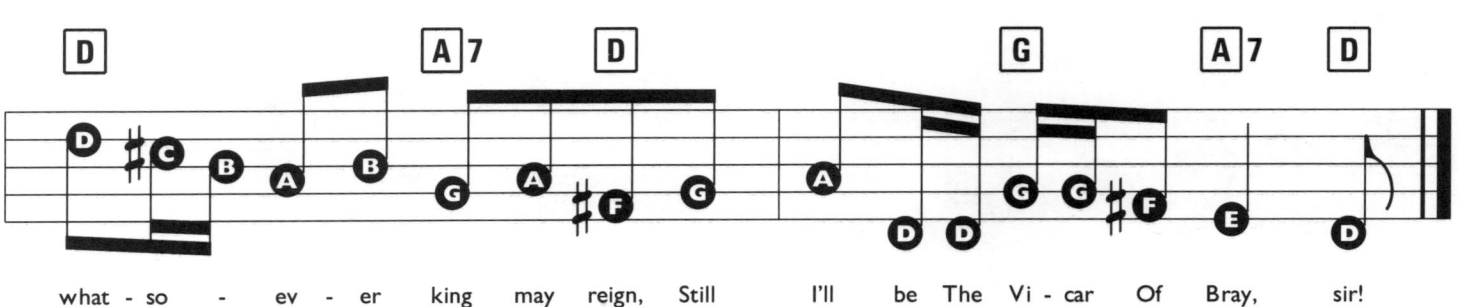

There Is A Tavern In The Town

Traditional.

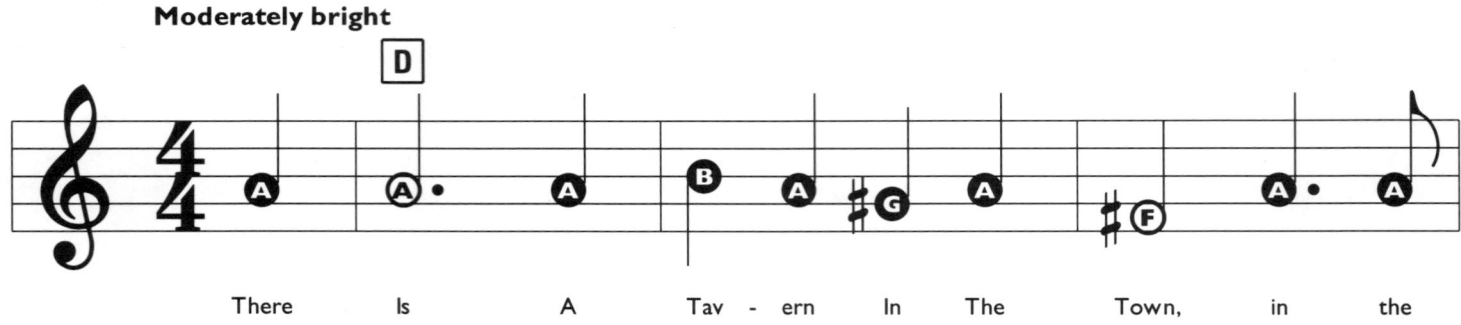

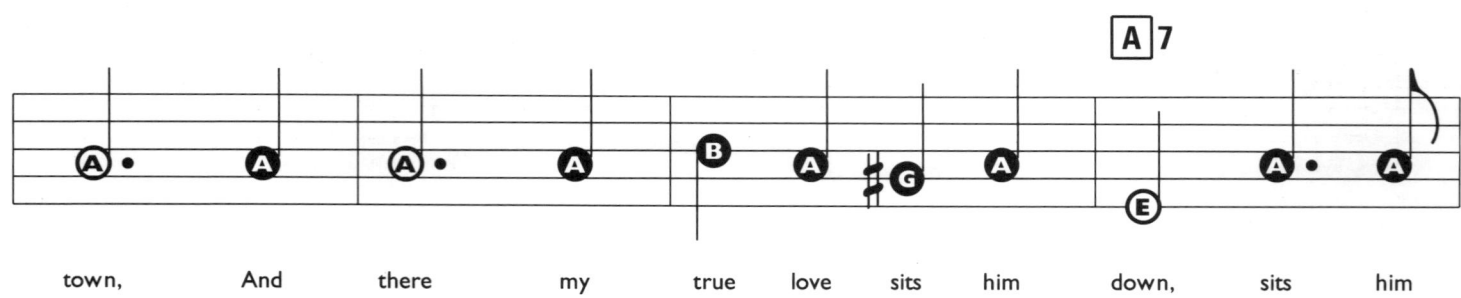

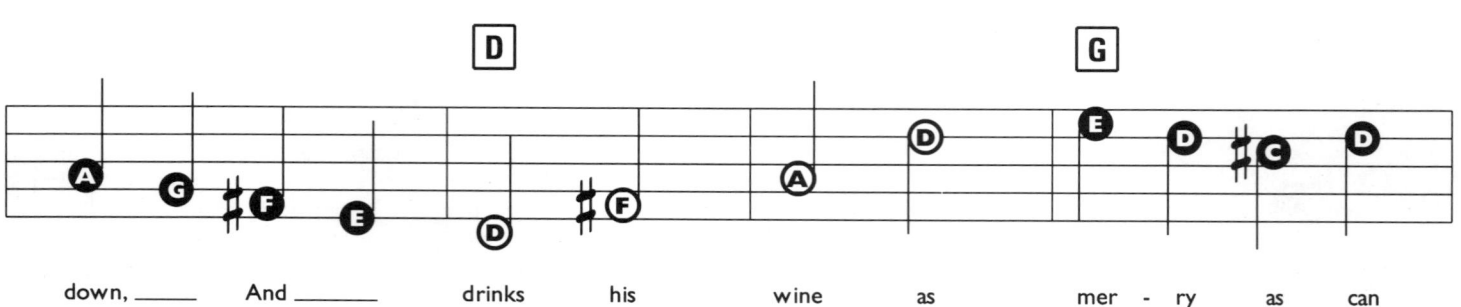

© Copyright 1993 Dorsey Brothers Music Limited, 8/9 Frith Street, London W1.
All Rights Reserved. International Copyright Secured.

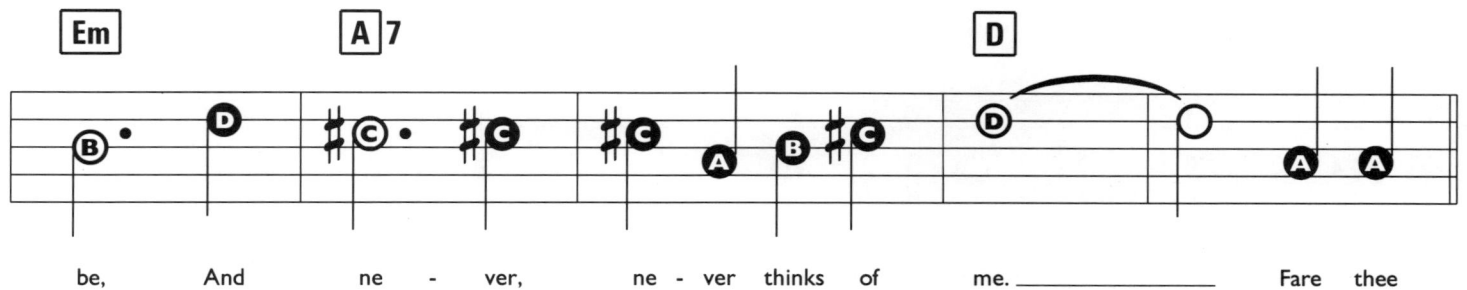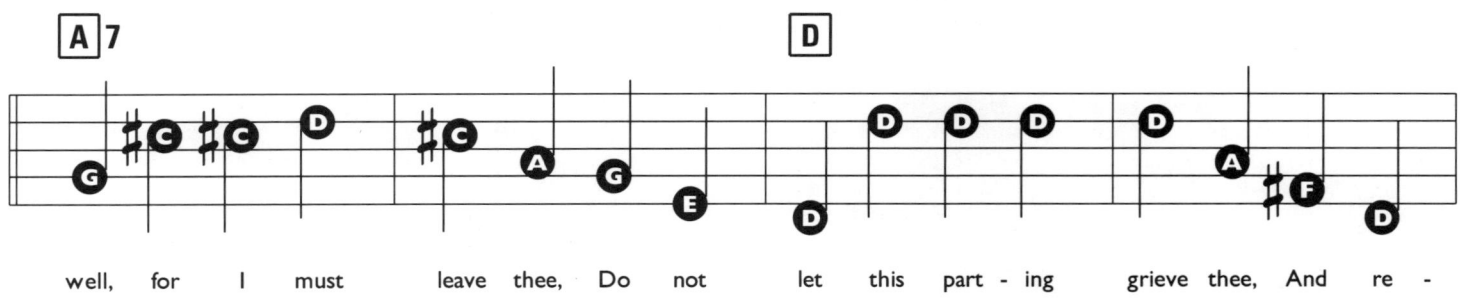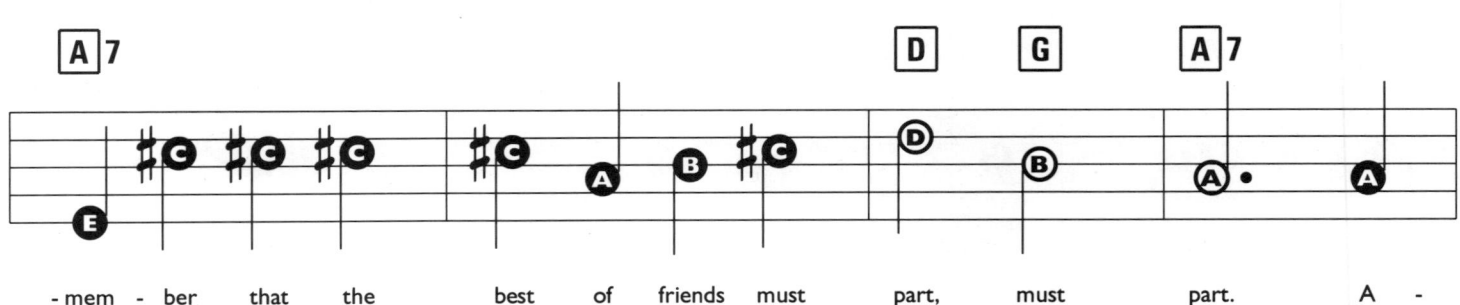

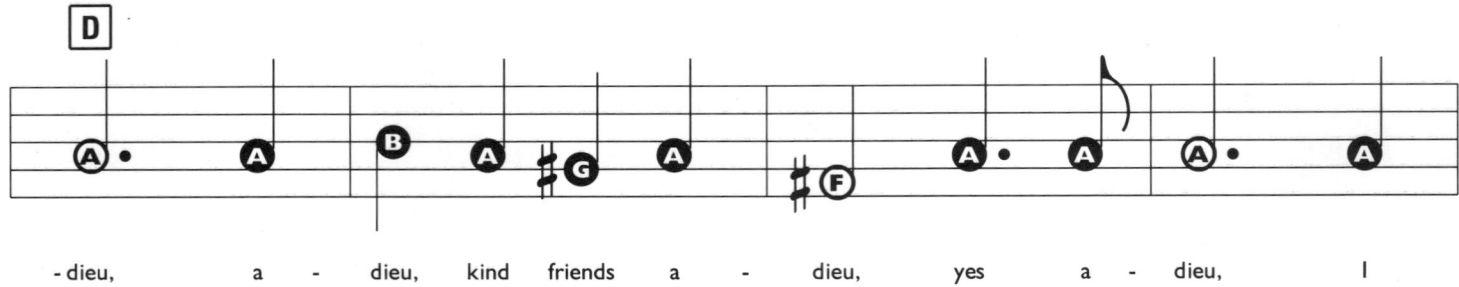
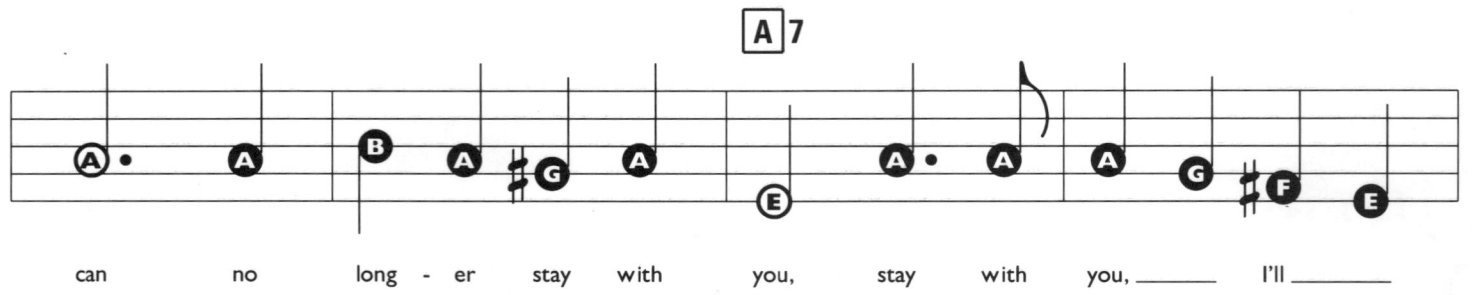
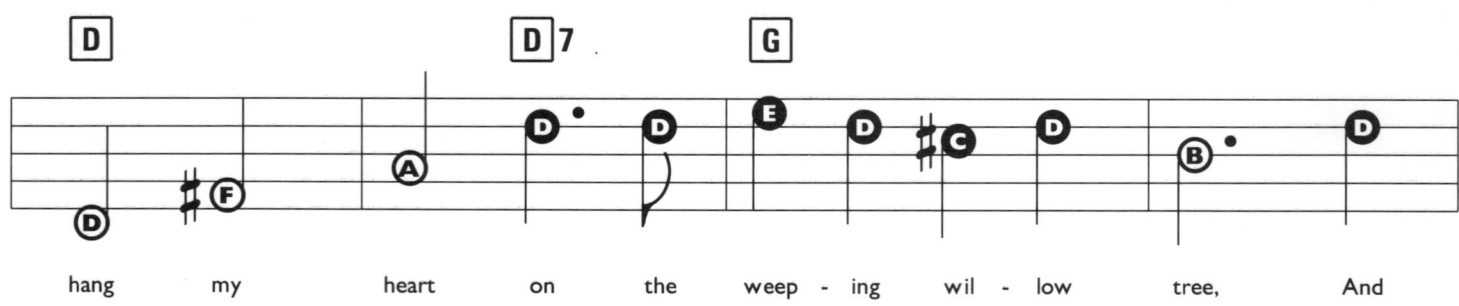
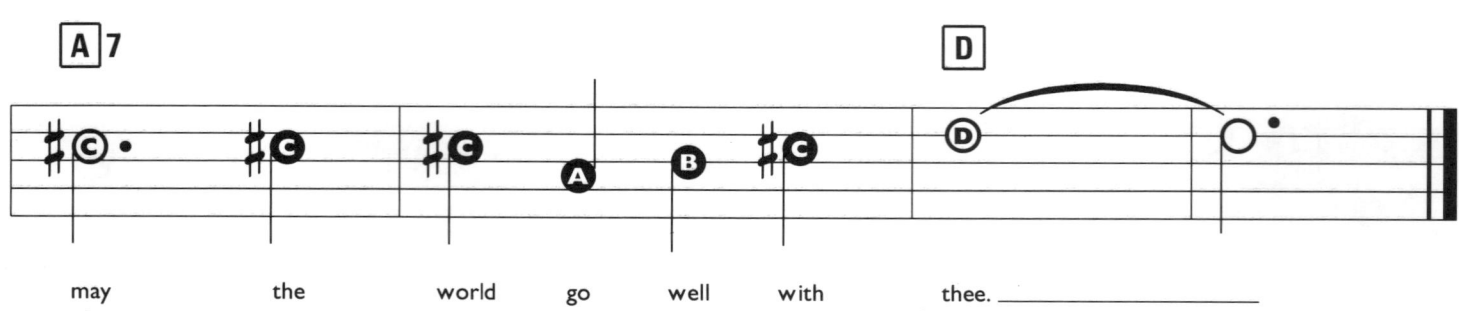